Good Church / Bad Church

A Look into the Evangelical Church Community

Fred Herschelman

ISBN 979-8-89112-308-3 (Paperback)
ISBN 979-8-89112-309-0 (Digital)

Covenant Books
11661 Hwy 707
Murrells Inlet, SC 29576
www.covenantbooks.com

"The good news is in Christ alone in him, not the idea of him."
—Pastor Matt Purvis, Grassroots
Community Church, Hawaii

"God pulled me out of the church that I was at to reach the people."
—Pastor James Tanaka, Hawaii

"It is not about being inclusive or being conservatives or republicans, but about being transformed by the glory of God…Our hope is not in this nation, but in Christ."
—Pastor Chris Promersberger, Mountain
Valley Church, New Mexico

"There is a biblical formula that can be followed, but a lot of people do not want to follow it."
—Reverend Guzman, Crossroads
Presbyterian Church, Delaware

"The constitution for a church needs to be the New Testament."
—Dr. John Goetsch, Author and Pastor of
Lancaster Baptist Church, California

"We need to rebuild trust in presenting the gospel message and actually go out and proclaim it."
—Pastor Brad Borowski, Living
Stones Network, Nevada

"If those that are supposed to protect you are working against you, a decision has to be made if you are going to obey an earthly king or the King of Kings…While fear is contagious, courage can also be contagious."
—Pastor Artur Pawlowski,
Street Church, Alberta

"What would happen if pastors prepared God's people for works of service so that 'ministry amateurs' did the work of ministry because they loved Jesus, instead of paid professionals?"

—Pastor Todd Petty, Christ's Church and Hillside Discipleship Church, Michigan

"The word of God is sufficient, we do not need extra Biblical rules. He does not want sacrifices, he wants you. While God does get jealous and angry, he is ultimately a God of Love. He loves you."

—Pastor Ryan Glosson, First Baptist Church Turbeville, South Carolina

"The church does not help when it claims God says when he does not, or that God does not say when he does."

—Pastor Ross Shannon, First Baptist Church of Lapeer

"The greatest danger that we see in the church today is silence. Silence about church, silence about false teachings, and silence about truth. We need Jesus as savior but also as Lord...but be careful, because the goats are feeding amongst the sheep."

—Pastor Henry Bechthold, Author and Retired Pastor, Minnesota

"I had to come to terms with the reality that there were people out there calling themselves pastors of Christ's sheep and were teaching them such deception."

—Pastor John Glenn, Amazing Grace Baptist Church, Hawaii

"Oftentimes when someone privileged comes into a situation to help out the unprivileged, there is sometimes a subconscious superiority mentality to it...What would it look like if we are all doing this together, as one, with no superiority."

—Pastor Leo Robinson, Good Church, Flint, Michigan

Contents

1

The Journey

The woman sat in the audience as the pastor artfully crafted his message. Today the speaker would not be focusing on biblical truths, exegetical preaching, or reflecting on the teachings of Christ. He had another mission in mind, a higher calling of sorts for today. His gestures became more animated, he started talking quicker, and his movements got more excited as his speech became more passionate. He needed to make sure that the people were on his side, so he had to engage in the full plethora of emotional experiences. He knew that he had loyalty; many of his loyal henchmen had long since abandoned serving Christ and pledged their loyalty to him. But not everybody had done so. This woman in particular did not and had the audacity to suggest that the pastor take a more biblical approach to the church and his sermons. So the pastor carried on using the full force and authority of the pulpit to authoritatively declare his message and wage war against this person who dared to speak against his religious institution.

I watched the woman run out of the church crying. Apparently, she could not sit in her seat any longer. While the pastor did not mention her by name, it was apparent that everyone in the church knew who she was. I was not surprised. I had seen this type of thing before. Questioning a pastor or, even worse, pointing out the direction that the church was heading in could turn the wrath of the religious institution against you. Oftentimes these churches leave behind starved sheep that are left wandering the fields, looking for any type of substance, but are left wounded, limping, and bleeding as the church seeks to align herself with the world rather than Christ.

In other places, we see a stark contrast. A new image is being painted on a new portrait. There are robust and vibrant churches that are changing lives and the community, where families are healed and individuals are transformed. Powerful churches where faith is refreshed, lives are reconstructed, and members learn strong biblical truths that change themselves and their families and then go out and change the community. Churches that are anchored on biblical principles, which lead to transformed lives, families, and individuals. They breathe life into you and push you down paths of righteousness. These types of churches are not seeking instruction from Hollywood but, rather, the Bible as they seek to steer their ship toward the kingdom of God and not the kingdom of this world. They look more like the churches in Acts 2, rather than the decaying institutions that are just waiting to die. Robust and vibrant areas where the power of God is transforming lives and families are often referred to as healthy churches because they create healthy people and families. Individuals may provide the leadership, but a higher power is steering the ship.

But why the stark contrast? And what can be done to change it? This is a tough topic to address. Many pastors do not want to address it. There is a very real danger in being a cynic or a critic, to allowing negativity and hostility to impact your view. But there is also a very real danger in not saying anything, of allowing religion, distortion, and lies to alter and change what is supposed to be God's kingdom. Some churches are already good churches and on the right path. In this case, petty criticism is never helpful. Other churches are unhealthy, and silence is not always the best answer. In fact, silence can be construed as an endorsement and be dangerous. So how do you address this sensitive topic?

In America, racial relations can sometimes be a delicate topic. America is a melting pot of a variety of cultures and races; most families immigrated here at one point or another at some time. Most people understand that if one or two people or even a group of people from an ethnic group do something wrong, it is not necessarily indicative of an entire race. If you think an entire racial group is bad due to the actions of one person or a group of people, there is a term for you. You are a racist. The actions of a few people do not determine the actions of an entire race. There are good people and bad people as there are good churches and bad churches.

I travel for a living. I buy and sell distressed houses across America. I loved it and eventually abandoned my primary residence to travel full-time. Sometimes I stay at a place for a week, sometimes a month, sometimes a few months. My family comes with me. We have had the opportunity to visit great churches all across America, from up in Alaska by the Arctic circle, to the bottom of Florida in the Florida Keys, from Maine to the furthest point of Hawaii. During these travels, it was exciting to see many good, strong, healthy churches that are changing the community and run by great pastors; cities on a hill that are shining a bright light into darkness; and churches that bring food, healthcare, love, and the gospel into the community. There are certainly a lot of good churches across America.

The journey was interesting. Our family was able to cross geographical, cultural, racial, economical, and most importantly, denominational lines. We have been to small churches, big churches, historically rich churches to new churches with no history, churches in wealthy areas to churches in poverty-stricken areas, and English-speaking churches and Spanish-speaking churches.

We have seen a lot. From an Easter in Nashville, Tennessee, with the hustle, bustle, and excitement and driving past one massive megachurch building after another, to small little churches holding a few people that still need a little paint and drywall. From churches where they softly hum hymns during worship to churches where they jump up and down, dance, shout, and praise! Regardless of your worship style, sometimes you cannot help but get caught up in the enthusiasm of the moment. From wealthy churches with large buildings to small churches that might not even have their own building.

There have of course been a plethora of theological and stylistic differences. Some churches are more charismatic and some churches are more cessationists. We sat in churches that had different views of salvation. Some aligned more with Calvinism and others with Arminians. Eschatology, or end-time beliefs, are all across the board. There are arguments about whether Christ raptures His church before, during, or after the tribulation. Some churches do not even believe a rapture will take place. Some churches have a very contemporary feel to them with the best and latest sound systems, a clean and modern building, to the latest and greatest in visual aids; some are even in a mall or storefront. Others are in a more traditional church and have spent less time focusing on visual aesthetics.

Sometimes the differences in worship styles, climate, theology, and geographical locations can create a dramatic difference. But this book is not going to focus as much on the differences between the churches but rather on the truth that ties them together. Are there any essential doctrines that churches have to agree with? And if so, are there some nonessential doctrines that people can just agree to disagree on? One thing I have noticed is that when someone leaves a church to go to a different church, the friends they made at a previous church generally drop off. Oftentimes when visiting new churches, you can get recruited from enthusiastic members. "Our church has this program and this program." "Come meet the pastor." "Look at our new facilities!" Should it be like that, or are we all one in the body of Christ? Are some enthusiastic members eagerly building their own kingdoms instead of God's kingdom? And what is a good church, and what would one even look like?

So this book will talk about some of the differences between these churches, whether they are cultural, theological, or just different mentalities and worship styles. Can all these churches be more united? Should we be more united? But as the title implies, what about bad churches? Is there even such a thing? Are all churches automatically good and all pastors automatically good pastors? Does just putting a sign up that says you are a church make you automatically in the body of Christ and under God's protection? Is there even anything such as a bad church, and is that possible? I think history provides us with the most dramatic example of a bad church, and we can see this in Germany.

Before the second World War, approximately 98 percent of Germany was affiliated with the church. Germany was religious, as this was the land of Martin Luther. But that 98 percent number is a deceiving statistic as almost all children were baptized from birth into the church, and most people never bothered to leave the church, even though the church played no part in many lives. However, there still was a strong undercurrent of faith for many, even if it was just for cultural and traditional reasons for some.

The church was a part of the people, part of the lives, part of that culture. But theological liberalism had invaded the church, and the congregants would decide which parts of the Bible were true and which were not, different ideas were explored, and the philosophers and scientists took precedence over biblical truth, weakening the faith for many. Christianity was embedded in the culture, but this was not a life-changing faith; it was just a part of their tradition and was not penetrating their hearts, minds, or beliefs.

It was this Germany that was ready for a new leader to take over, and that leader would be Adolf Hitler. While Adolf Hitler came into power through the democratic process, it was not long before the democratic process was abandoned, and Hitler had complete control over everything, schools, institutions, businesses, the government, and most importantly, the church. Hitler loved the church, as long as it was him that controlled and manipulated it. Hitler's original plan with the church was to "wage war against it."[1] The Nazi regime created the Nazi Master Plan: the Persecution of the Christian Churches.[2] But Hitler never got around to directly attacking the church; instead, he decided to lead and take control of it. While he would rail and write about his hatred for Christianity in his private time and make vows to his friends on how he would eliminate it, he was a politician, so for the public, he would oftentimes mention Christianity or God in his speeches or quotes.

---

[1] Richard Weikart, *Hitler's Religion: The Twisted Beliefs That Drove the Third Reich* (Washington, DC: Regnery History, 2016), 7.

[2] Ray Comfort, *Hitler, God and the Bible.* (Washington: WND Books, 2012), 130.

Hitler coined the term *positive Christianity* to reflect his views. Positive Christianity eliminated sin, salvation, and Christ's death and resurrection and replaced it with some of the positive aspects of Christianity that Hitler enjoyed. He eliminated the entire Old Testament as he saw it as a Jewish book. In *Mein Kampf*, Hitler presented Jesus as a whip-bearing savior sent to stand against the Jews who eventually killed him. Hitler incorporated his own writings and ideologies into the church. *The Thirty-Point Program for the National Reich Church* stated that the church was established absolutely and exclusively in the service of but one doctrine: race and nation.

The Bible and other Christian publications would not be imported into Germany. The National Reich Church made it its duty to use all its energy to popularize Hitler's book, *Mein Kampf*; all the altars had *Mein Kampf*, the most sacred book to the German nation and God. To the left of the altar would be a sword, and all crucifixes must be cleared away to make way for the swastika. Some verses, such as Romans 13:1–2, about being subject to governing authorities, were pushed. It was made clear that

> The National Reich Church does not acknowledge forgiveness of sins. It represents the standpoint in which it will always proclaim that a sin once committed will be ruthlessly punished by the honorable and indestructible laws of nature and punishment will follow during the sinners' lifetime.[3]

The German Christian movement rose up alongside Hitler's positive Christianity and rooted itself in the Protestant movement. They published their own catechism and their own version of the Bible called *The Message of God*. This version of the Bible completely abandoned the entire Old Testament and just heavily paraphrased fragments of the New Testament. Jesus was portrayed as a human warrior fighting the evils of his day. The Sabbath was changed to a

---

[3]   Ibid., 120–124

holiday, the Sermon on the Mount eliminated any blessing for the merciful, and the Ten Commandments were replaced by twelve new commandments. "Honor your Fuhrer and master"[4] became the new eleventh commandment.

Hitler expanded beyond the church and eliminated the previous holidays of Christmas and Easter and added new holidays. Gun control laws and regulations were implemented to prevent hunting accidents. State identification cards were issued; freedom of speech was limited as individual liberties were sacrificed for the good of the country. Businesses became entwined with so many rules and regulations that they could not function as people had less control over their individual lives. Controlling the church allowed Hitler to control all of society. Most of the pastors went along; they were put on the government's payroll after all. There were a few holdouts; Dietrich Bonhoeffer was one of those pastors who would not submit to the Nazi regime, fought Hitler, and was later killed for those beliefs. But his writings would influence other generations after him to stand for truth and fight for righteousness.

So history shows us an extreme example of a bad church with nazified Germany. Fortunately, we do not have anything as bad as this in America today. Nothing is this extreme. But do we have bad churches or at least churches that could be better? Some may think the term *unhealthy church* is a more accurate fit. In this book, we will be referring to the church as a particular building or group of buildings, as most Americans do. From a biblical perspective, the word *church* is translated from the Greek word *ekklesia*, meaning an assembly or the called-out ones. So we have the universal church, which is everyone, everywhere, who has a personal relationship with Jesus Christ. Paul refers to the church in their house, not a church building, but rather a body of believers. All those who have received salvation through faith in Jesus Christ comprise the universal church. It is everybody. Everyone who has received salvation in Christ Jesus.

---

4   Russell Grigg, "Choose Country." Creation.com | Creation Ministries International. Accessed February 10, 2020. https://creation.com/hitler-bible.

Then we have the local church. Paul spent much of his time writing to the local churches, which compose a large part of the New Testament. The local church would be the individual church buildings that you see when you drive around. So we have the universal church which consists of all God's people, the body of Christ, throughout all history, which cannot be found in a building or a denomination. And then we have the local church, which may or may not be a part of the universal church. It is the local church that we will generally be referencing in this book.

It has been said that there are basically three groups of pastors. The first group is composed of pastors who love people, have strong biblical doctrine, and rely on God to lead and direct them. There is no major error in their doctrine or blatant unrepentant sin in their personal lives. They run good churches. The second group is basically like the first group, but they might have picked up some type of theory or doctrinal point at some point, likely from listening to another pastor online or through a book. They thought this was correct, but it was not. They did not know any better. They are still a good church and will correct those errors when they realize their mistake. The third group is different from the first two; they want nothing to do with the truth.[5] They intentionally twist what the Bible actually says to what they want the Bible to say, whether this is for wealth, ego, or just because. They are not a good church. This is what we will be looking at in this book, and if some of these pastors are starting to create a new movement, a movement that is polluting the body of Christ. A new movement that is redefining the very definition of Christianity.

In the New Testament, the Bible places a strong emphasis on truth. Paul, the Bereans, and Jesus and the disciples were consistently warning us about being deceived and to focus on finding the truth. False teaching is warned about in every book in the New Testament with the exception of Philemon. There are over one hundred verses in the New Testament warning us about false teaching and those that twist the truth, and the Old Testament is littered with countless

---

[5]   Quote from Pastor Keith Atwood who is introduced later in the book.

examples. Is it possible that we might have false teaching in some local churches today? Are they polluting the body of Christ? In some cases, this may be the case, but we can take solace that God will purify His church.

> And I tell you, you are Peter, and on this
> rock I will build my church, and the gates of hell
> shall not prevail against it.[6]

Across America, many people have stopped going to church in the wake of COVID. Many churches are still running with half of a congregation than what they had previously. I have met people from many different states who used to go to church but no longer do. There are different types of reasons. Some have drifted into apostasy or wandered from the faith. But others still have a robust and vibrant faith that includes daily prayer and Bible reading. They want to go to a good church but cannot find any in the area. Maybe they were wounded in the church from some type of religious trauma. Some are deeply scarred. Others have left because their feelings have been hurt. Some have left as they felt the church was not adding any value to their lives. Some recognized that what the church was saying did not match up with the Bible. Some no longer wanted to be controlled by an institution but wanted to find freedom in Christ. A lot of people tried to find a good, healthy church, but after driving around for so many Sundays, they finally gave up. They may be frustrated, lost, and discouraged, but they have not given up their faith yet.

This book does not go around and classify, categorize, and catalog all the churches in America to sort all the good churches and bad churches. It does not hold one denomination or type of church over another. There was no litmus test created to classify churches. Hundreds of churches in every state in America were either visited, researched, or interviewed. Thirty pastors from good churches across America were then selected to interview on the attributes of a good church. The pastors selected are very unique and interesting pastors;

---

[6] Matthew 16:18 (ESV)

some are not nationally known. Some have not yet been properly introduced across America. And not all of the pastors may have universally agreed on all the points presented by each pastor, but rather, each pastor presented their own unique aspect of what makes a good church. Together, they help create a clear picture of what a good church looks like. All these unique perspectives from across America help create a vivid painting. Maybe not of a perfect church, but of what a good, healthy, strong church does look like.

In many cases, American churches can be a case of extremes. One church may be small while another is huge. One church might silently hum hymns while another dances and shouts. One church may be harbored in the business and bustle of a large city while another is set among the countryside. But it is in the balance where we find the Prince of Peace.

There are old distressed houses that need work and have been abandoned across America. Sometimes you look at a house, and you just want to demolish it. And in some cases, that is needed. But in other cases, if you can just fix the roof, you have a good start, and then remove all the damaged or moldy drywall and items, update the plumbing, structure, and electrical, and then install new drywall and flooring. Change out the bathroom fixtures and cabinets, paint the house, update the fixtures, and then you have a new and restored house. Oftentimes, this new house bears no resemblance to what it once was. The same thing can be applied to the church. Quitting the church and giving up is easy; that can be done and is being done. But what about fixing it? Can the church be restored? And how do you go about that? And what do some of the pastors from good churches all across America have to say about it?

2

The Blending

Across the Pacific Ocean lies the furthest Western State of America, Hawaii. Joining America in 1959 as the fiftieth state, it may be able to stake a claim as the most unique state in the United States. With its beautiful geography, ideal climate, and great beaches, it is mostly known as a vacation destination. But this is home to 1.4 million people. Here, you will find a mix of Native Hawaiians, relocated mainlanders, and those from all around the world who now call the islands home. You have a blending of different cultures, ethnicities, ideas, and religions. While you might be able to drive across most states in the course of a day, in Hawaii, you would have to take multiple airplane rides to get across this state.

In Honolulu, we have the big city and the hustle and bustle of all American big busy cities, just with more scenic views. But when you get to the Big Island, things get different; it marches to the beat of its own drum. Kona and Hilo entrap most of the tourists, Kona with its sun and beaches, and Hilo with the jungle and waterfalls. But outside those areas, you get introduced to Hawaiian time, and you better learn how to adjust. Hawaiians have their own hand signals, phrases, terms, mentality, and way of doing life, which differentiates them from the tourists. It is American, and sometimes it is not. You either adjust and fit in or it spits you out. The easiest way to explain it is that sometimes it feels more like being in another country, than actually being in another country.

As Hawaii is unique to America, the Big Island is unique to Hawaii. It has eight different climate zones—lava and flowers, desert, and rainforest. You can go snow skiing on the top of Mauna Kea in the morning and then go surfing in the afternoon. In the center of this uniqueness lies Pahoa. If you never had a chance to live in the 1960s and wanted to, just visit Pahoa. In downtown Pahoa, the buildings are eccentric and colorful, as are the people. Unique and unconventional hippies roam the streets. Some are playing the guitar, maybe riding a unicycle, with tie-dyed shirts, no shirts, long hair, and no hair. One may have a pet dog, another a pet chicken. The smell of the jungle and the distant ocean breeze mix with incense and marijuana. These are the nonconformers of society, those who are not going to follow everyone else and live life according to their own rules.

In the center of Pahoa lies Grassroots Community Church, another nonconformer. It is a bakery during the week, then shuts down on Sunday to host a church service. Pastor Matt Purvis preaches in the center of spiritual chaos. Since Hawaii is the melting pot of cultures, it is also the melting pot of Religions, and it seems that they all fuse together here. In Pahoa, Christianity is welcome here, but in many cases, it is a version that also blends with Buddhism, Hinduism, and lots of New Age ideas. Yoga, enlightenment, karma, and the cross are all mixed together. Religious syncretism, or the blending of religions, is very common here. Many people here are searching for the truth, but there is a lot of confusion. Multiple religions are explored, multiple paths and bits and pieces from all these religions and ideas get jumbled up, mixed together, and presented in a big bag of disorientation, which looks different for each person.

But instead of teaching about reincarnation, Pastor Matt teaches on the atonement. Instead of teaching Samsara, the resurrection is presented. Instead of preaching Enlightenment, true enlightenment from the Bible is presented. Nirvana is abandoned to show the path to true eternal life. Karma is looked at through the lens of the Bible and scripture and the real Guru, Jesus, is presented. When asked how he survives amid this spiritual chaos, Pastor Matt reminds us that every religion has to find some way to Christ. He is the best teacher, the most known, and the most famous. He is already incorporated into all these other religions. He has to be addressed somehow. So it makes sense to put Him in their storyline. The world has to have some answers; He does not need one. Grasping at straws to make Christ on your side, but we do not need to form Him into our religion, we need to be formed in His image.

Pastor Matt Purvis stated that a lot of people do not understand why it cannot be this way or why it cannot be that way. They want Jesus to fit into their lifestyle. But the real gospel cannot live besides false things; it is not compatible with false things. It is the person of Jesus, not just Him. It is not just that He was the best teacher; He particularly did something that we cannot. We can be like Him, but we really cannot, ever. There are a lot of phrases out there, "What would Jesus do?" and "Be like Jesus," and we should strive for that. But we really cannot be like Him. He was unique. He made the sacrifice. You have to be in Christ, not just the idea of Him and not just the circumstances of Him.

Speaking of the sacrifice, Pastor Matt stated:

> There are a lot of bad ideas of what Christ accomplished at the cross and his life, theories of the atonement or really bad ideas. There is the mystical idea of the atonement of Christ consciousness, that he can be found in the trees and the seas, prevalent in Hawaii. The concept that Christ's life, death, and resurrection is an example, an example to be a morally good person and we should follow that example. And then the Jesus died on the cross just to show you how much God loves you, God loves you so much that there is no price he wouldn't pay to have you back, he was willing to give everything for us and in so by giving his son we will soften our hearts and bend our knees and say God I did not know you loved me so much, I'm going to come to you now. There is some truth to it, but it still falls

short of what Christ accomplished, in him we
have redemption through his blood- the forgiveness of our trespasses according to the riches of
his Grace…It goes far beyond showing us God's
love, which is true…These other ideas are popular because they skip over our true condition…
The good news is in Christ alone in him, not the
idea of him.

Love is a commonly used word in Pahoa. You even see it tagged on the sides of buildings, on shirts, or used in phrases. But Pastor Matt reminds us that we do not even know what love is; we learn it from God. The love in Puna, and to a lesser extent in our culture, is really about acceptance. Tolerance. We need to be accepted. But the ultimate love is not accepting who you are. The ultimate love is the sacrifice made by Christ. This helps us understand love more thoroughly and more truthfully. We need to rescue those who do not know it, rescue those who deserve freedom.

"Those who do not know history are destined to repeat it." It is this study of history that Pastor James Tanaka likes to focus on. Pastor James preaches through history. He states that God pulled him out of the church that he was at, to reach the people. Instead of focusing on purchasing and maintaining a building, he goes to where the people are, at the beach. Pastor James sees all the answers to all the spiritual problems can be found in history. Hawaii does have a unique history, and you can see it today. In some of the rural areas, the locals may acknowledge that America runs the show, but they pledge their allegiance to the Kingdom of Hawaii. After all, this was their own nation-state, until being annexed by America. But some-thing exciting happened here.

In the nineteenth century, out of this island in the Pacific, one of the largest revivals we have ever seen shook the soil of this nation. It started in Hilo when a group of missionaries were able to share the gospel message with some of the locals. One of the local women acknowledged that she had killed some of her babies as she did not want them anymore. She was sorrowful and cried out in repentance.

This sparked a chain reaction, and other women repented. Pretty soon, a majority of the island was turning to Christ. This started in the Hilo area and still retains a large Christian presence.

Pastor James believes that to maintain the purity of the Christian faith and avoid blending in with the other faiths, or religious syncretism, you have to be embedded in the truth, which uses the Bible as our foundational source. He has found the formula for the greats of the past, and he uses these formulas to revive people today. He tells stories of the adventures of Titus Coan. Titus was a missionary who helped work the great revivals that were sweeping New England. When he left America to arrive at the Kingdom of Hawai'i, it was a different world and culture than what he came from. He arrived amid utter immorality with the family institution hardly known.[7] When Titus Coan arrived, the island's size was rapidly shrinking due to the custom of killing a lot of the infants. What Coan did not realize is that some of the groundwork was already completed for him. A group of missionaries had arrived previously and started an earnest prayer network for the locals. Titus Coan believed in following the formulas that were used in previous revivals—extraordinary prayer, consecutive meetings, learning the language and culture of the people, counseling, and preaching the Word of God. Titus found this formula from other revivals and believed it would be the foundation for future ones.

Titus Coan would go on frequent and lengthy preaching tours walking up to one hundred miles from home to preach to people three to five times per day. The conviction of sin was intense during these preaching tours. There was a public confession of sin and great joy in deliverance. People started repenting in great multitudes. Deep conviction, repentance, and changed lives were multiplying across the island. Public confessions with pleas for forgiveness were common. People were traveling great distances to hear the Word of God. A revival was underway. Titus Coan had a detailed follow-up system that he used to keep track of everyone's spiritual progress and

---

7   B. Feet, *1836 Hawaiian Revival*. Beautiful Feet (2018, November 27), https://romans1015.com/1836-hawaiian-revival/.

account for wandering members. He also believed in church discipline and suspended people for notorious sins.[8]

The small town of Hilo grew from one thousand to ten thousand people, as people wanted to live closer to the Hilo church to hear the Bible being taught.[9] Pastor James likes to tell stories of mass baptisms, using Hilo Bay to hold large crowds. A deep reverence for God was installed in the people as they abandoned sin to turn to the Word of God. David B. Lyman and Lorenzo Lyons helped bring in the harvest. Three-quarters of the population was transformed. Thieves restored property, drunks quit drinking, marriages were restored, and relationships were reconciled. The faith not only penetrated the people; it transformed the government. King Kamehameha III made Christianity the established religion on the island. He established the nation's motto, which is still the motto for the state today: "The life of the land is perpetuated in righteousness." This was a far cry from a people group that once saw Kane as the god of light, Ku as the god of war, Pele as the goddess of fire and volcanoes, and Haumea as the Hawaiian fertility goddess. By the time Titus Coan retired, he had baptized close to sixteen thousand people and seen many more lives transformed. The pagan kingdom of Hawaii was now a Christian nation.

The blending of religions or adding certain elements of other religions to the Christian faith is not just found in Hawaii but can be found in pockets all across America. Pastor Chris Promersberger can be found in the state of New Mexico, just east of Albuquerque. It is here where old Native American religious beliefs still find their way into Christianity, or Christianity finds its way into Native American beliefs. These beliefs started colliding when the Europeans and Native Americans clashed in the new world, but they are still prevalent today. Pastor Chris comes from where they have a lot of different

---

8   "The Adventures of Titus Coan," pp 65 and 68, *Life in Hawaii: An Autobiographical Sketch of Mission Life and Labors (1835–1881)*, Revised 2nd Edition (Copyright @ 2013, scriptoria books, Mesa, Arizona, USA).

9   G. T. Ministries, (n.d.). *1835–1840*, "Hawaii's Great Awakening: 1835–1840. Titus Coan and Revival," retrieved February 22, 2023, from https://www.gospeltruth.net/hawaii_revival.htm.

Native American populations. There are old missions and old pueblo Catholic missions. At one particular mission, there is still an old circular pot in the ground from when the Native Americans used to do sacrifices; the local Catholic church kept it for convenience.

Pastor Chris warns us about keeping images and idols around, no matter how meaningless they may see; they mean something. There are a lot of spiritualists out there. He is in a very pluralistic syncretized area. He noted that the area that he lives in sometimes looks more like it was cut from a scene in *Breaking Bad*, rather than an actual city. It is less about being an organized church and more about meditation, being one with the world, one with yourself. There are people involved in Wicca and the occult; they go off into the woods and hold seances. These Native American religions along with Wicca and elements of the occult fuse together with the Catholic church. He reminds us not to take symbols from the occult and have them as decorations in the house. Catholic statues are portrayed in a Native American style which is more cultural, more decoration. Various decorations, ornaments, and trinkets that blend old Native American tributes to various gods and possibly a hybrid with an old Catholic statue can be found in many houses and buildings in the area.

One challenge that Pastor Chris runs into as a gospel-preaching, Bible-believing church is the idea that you are not being inclusive; someone else is more inclusive. And that is common today. He reminds us that it is not about being inclusive or being Conservatives or Republicans but about being transformed by the glory of God. He says some Christian nationalists could have a tendency to get wrapped up in that, but he reminds us that our hope is not in this nation but in Christ. He struggles with having to do this in practical terms and living in the world but being on mission in the world.

Some solutions that he sees is putting a strong emphasis on elders teaching and weeding out some of these problems. But the biggest solution is being a praying, teaching, and word-centered church. Try to live by the standards of God's word. The main thing they have done is to help people grow and not separate discipleship from evangelism. One problem he sees is that if you go out and evangelize, then count a convert as a victory and stop there, and do not disciple; you have someone who will eventually fall through the cracks. Failing to correctly disciple new people will not lead to long-term results; it just brings bodies into the church. Step 1 is evangelization and step 2 is discipleship, and do not forget the second step.

Pastor Chris says that being a good church is a simple answer but difficult to put into practice. But it centers on faithfulness, repenting, and reading God's word. Teach substitutionary atonement. People are saved by faith alone. Christians should care because it is a matter of life and death; others should care as it defines love because God is love. You cannot change sanctification to self-improvement. This is contrary to the gospel; it is of the world. He reminds us that in Galatia, they got off on the wrong track with false gospels, and today, we can get off track with false gospels.

Pastor Chris says to remember 1 Corinthians 15, which says in part:

> Hold fast to the word I preached to you—unless you believed in vain. For I delivered to you as of first importance what I also received: that Christ died for our sins in accordance with the Scriptures, that he was buried, that he was raised on the third day in accordance with the Scriptures, and that he appeared to Cephas, then to the twelve.[10]

Pastor Chris reminds us that a good church leads to faithfulness in the gospel, and to guard against people twisting and distorting the gospel, you must first know it.

---

[10] Excerpt of 1 Corinthians 15:2b–5 (ESV)

3

Is Something Missing?

Today, in some churches, we can find a variety of sermon topics, "Dealing with Negative Thoughts," "Letting Go of Control," "Become What You Believe," or "Your Right Time Is Coming." You can focus on how to be a better leader, overcoming your obstacles, or listening to a series on love. They are all structured so that you can become the best you that you can be. The church's version of a modern day is how you can win friends and influence people seminar. And it sells well. Television shows are seen by millions of people, and it puts millions of dollars in the bank. Books are published, such as *Your Best Life Now: 7 Steps to Living at Your Full Potential* which quickly rose to number 1 on the self-help bestseller list and has sold more than one hundred million copies, and was on the *New York Times* Best Seller list for one hundred weeks. Americans are obsessed about how we can all become better versions of ourselves as we "Become a Better You."

When you look at all this, you can quickly see a consistent theme. How the power of "I am," positive thinking, and declaring victory over yourself can help you to discover and unlock your unique abilities so that you can live a more productive, successful, and happier life. You can listen to stories from people across the globe who have turned their lives around by using the powers of this principle. You can learn how the power of "I am" can help you discover your unique abilities and lead a more productive and happier life. The focus is on how this version of Christianity can be used to help us, instead of seeing it as a means to transform others.

We have a few streams coming in and impacting this movement. One stream is the American culture at large that wants to focus on individual freedoms and personal victories and let people do their own thing as we slide into moral relativism. Then we have the drying up stream of the seeker-sensitive and attractional church movement that turned the focus of the church away from the cross and onto church growth, larger buildings, and bigger stages, which in some areas ended up sacrificing truth for numbers. Then we have a third stream trickling in from some areas which is the Word of Faith movement.

The Word of Faith movement is spreading to churches across America. In its initial phase, you declare Bible verses over your life. It is repeatedly brought up that death and life are in the power of the tongue. And these are all great aspects, and if just left there, they can help out many people. Standing on the authority of the Bible is certainly beneficial, and champion athletes always think positively; an undefeated boxer never enters the ring thinking that he is going to lose. Watching your tongue, proclaiming truth, and speaking victory into your life can be very beneficial.

But some churches start to head in a new direction with this. They state that what you speak will come into existence, and that by speaking, you will control your own destiny. A system is created in which if you say the right words, eliminate negativity, and give the right amount of money, you will have the victorious life you dreamed of. God becomes more of a personal servant so that you can embark on your own personal adventure of being the best you that you can be.

In some more extreme cases, the positive proclamations can become a faith force that is used so we can become our own little gods ourselves. Some have even claimed that they do not need to pray to God; they can just pray to themselves. The greatest danger in some parts of the Word of Faith movement is not whether you can proclaim victory in your life or get a better job; it is that for many people, the message of Jesus is completely eliminated so that people can focus on themselves. The problem is when we change Christianity to suit our needs instead of allowing Christ to change us.

Rev. Guzman pastors a church out in Delaware. Delaware is a neat little state that is packed with a lot of fun. You can drive across it in a few hours. It has a lot of coastline and some nice beaches for how small the state is. Rev. Guzman likes to tell a story about Christopher Hitchens. Christopher Hitchens was a famous author who wrote the book *God Is not Great*. An articulate man, he was one of the more outspoken leaders of the new atheism movement and was against all religions in general. He held many debates on this subject. After one such debate in which he railed against Christianity and the people who believed in Christianity, a woman approached him. She stated, "Certainly, you could not be referring to me. I do not take the stories from the scripture literally." Do you make a distinction between fundamentalist faith and liberal religion? Hitchens responded that if you do not believe that Jesus of Nazareth was the Christ and Messiah and that He rose again from the dead and by His sacrifice, our sins are forgiven, you are not really in any meaningful sense a Christian.

And that really strikes at the heart of the issue. If your church is all about how you can be a better you, speak victory into your life, increase your finances, and overcome your obstacles and does not teach or address the gospel, you are not really a church, and not in any meaningful sense a Christian.

Rev. Josh Guzman is part of the PCA church, which broke away from the Presbyterian branch so that they could break away from the theological liberalism which is invading some churches. As a pastor, Rev. Guzman worries a lot about what he sees in other churches. He said that there is no seriousness in God's churches and that the problem is not just with liberal Christianity. There is a biblical formula that can be followed, but a lot of people do not want to follow it. That formula starts with the proclamation of the gospel every Sunday with the Word of God being preached.

Rev. Guzman says problems started with the church growth movement that really started in the '70s and focused on entertainment and fun programs, which turned the church more into a social club rather than a real church. It focused on entertainment while hiding the truth and the gospel message. It failed. People were not getting God's word in them. Today biblical illiteracy is at an all-time high, and we have no generational growth. Something is damaged. Some pastors are just worried about how to entertain people. Pastors who are not theologically minded want to take care of people and feed the sheep and might have a good heart, but those who cannot discern truth from error are not likely to help the sheep but rather let them feed on deception.

Rev. Guzman reminds us about the five solas of the reformation and the church needing to return to them: scripture alone, Christ alone, faith alone, grace alone, and the glory to God alone. He reminds us about church discipline which is biblically commanded and that the church must honor the glory of Christ, not look like the world, and deal with the corrosive effect of sin. He reminds us of the example in 1 Corinthians 5:1–2. He says that with unrepentant sin, particularly that which is public in nature or gross theological error, you should first seek to admonish and reclaim such a person. If that does not work, "let him who has done this be removed from among you."[11]

He reminds us that this is not a club; it is a missional identity. We have the acts that the church has always been charged with and the great commission, which has a global element. This needs to be carried out globally, but particularly in the West which has been blessed with money, learning, and education, putting America in a position for effective global missions. Well-meaning churches who would call themselves evangelical do not generally stand up and preach from the scriptures and do not engage in expository preaching. They generally preach topical messages focused on self-improvement rather than focusing on the essential truths of the faith.

Reverend Guzman reminds us that contending with heresy is not something new; it is an age-old problem. Paul had to contend with heresy and false teaching, and the church has collectively denounced false teaching in the beginning within the first five hundred years. It did not go away after that. Denouncing false teachings

---

[11]   1 Corinthians 5:2b (ESV)

and false teachers is the way that it will be to the very end; they sow disunity and false doctrine, not trust. It is not just the other world religions that we have to worry about but those under the doctrine of Christianity. Doctrinal faithfulness to the scriptures is important. People have to be in context with what the Bible is being taught and is teaching. And the gospel needs to be proclaimed every Sunday.

Toward the opposite end of the country, Dr. John Goetsch is based out of California and trains pastors and is also an evangelist, author, and teacher. Dr. John Goetsch is the author of the *Saviour Sensitive Church*, which addressed the differences between a savior-sensitive church and a seeker-sensitive church and the snares of postmodernism in the culture and church at large. He outlined how to leave the seeker-sensitive format and become a Christ-centered or savior-sensitive church. He reminds us that the seeker-sensitive format which left Christ and the gospel out of the church has failed, and we cannot leave remnants of this movement behind. We need to exalt Christ.

Dr. Goetsch states that the constitution for a church needs to be the New Testament. Jesus is the head of the church and empowers the church. We need to follow the New Testament principles when Jesus formed the church. He refers to Matthew 16:18 which states,

> And I tell you, you are Peter, and on this
> rock I will build my church, and the gates of hell
> shall not prevail against it.[12]

Dr. Goetsch says that we need to focus on the New Testament and creating the environment to preach and teach God's word. The foundation needs to be the Word of God. Look at the early church in Acts, which had doctrine, fellowship, breaking of bread, and prayer meetings. A church should be an oasis from the world. The world is going to attack with its own doctrines, so the church needs to be a shelter from the world, and a Christian needs to belong to an organization of fellow believers.

---

[12] Matthew 16:18 (ESV)

Dr. Goetsch says that if you have unsaved in your church, you need to share the gospel. He tells a story of sharing the gospel message in prison. At the start of the message, when he was talking about sin and the need for a savior, the people held their heads in shame. They were in prison; they knew they had sinned. But when he got to the good news that everyone who shall call upon the name of the Lord shall be saved, people started clapping and getting excited. There is power in the story of the cross and power in its freedom. Sometimes you have to get through the harsh part of the message to get to the good part.

Pastor Goetsch preaches in revival meetings and works with other pastors for these events. He says that for a revival to happen, you have to look at the condition of the church. The early church had its own personality. You have to preach the gospel, hit a few nerves, and get a feel. Some churches are already in a state of revival, some are tired, some are worn out, and some are giving up. Some already gave up. Most Christians are living in fear and uncertainty. They need the power of God. God's way is the only way. Where God is, there will be power. Some churches are dying. What he tries to do is encourage the pastor, pray for him, get fire in his heart, put a spark in him, and light that fire. There is power in prayer, power behind prayer, and God's power. Prayer has always been the foundation behind any type of revival.

Pastor Goetsch stated that everyone wants change. Everyone wants different things and does not want to be old-fashioned. We are looking for new things and new programs. But God does not change. God has already shown us the formula. There is danger in pulling away from the Word of God. Be bold, and stick to what has been proven to work. It is important to know the needs of the audience, get a feel, and preach to those needs, but you must preach the word, and if you have unsaved, which you likely do, a preacher is responsible to share the gospel.

Be careful if something is needs-centered rather than Christ-centered. Many people come to church to feel positive, feel good, contribute, and be a part of the family and community. And this is good, but they need much more than to be a part of a family. They need to know that they have sinned, but more importantly, that there is a solution.

Pastor Goetsch reminds us that the devil counteracts everything. In the time of Nero, this was done with a sword. The enemy is going to attack God's work and destroy it by force. We are starting to see government overreach now. Churches are becoming oppressed. Satan is going to use the government. Critics attack and question the validity of the Bible from multiple places, schools, movies, government, etc. but stand on the truth of God's word. One hour a week in a good place does not work when the rest of the week, you are in the world. When the pen and media attack, return to the Bible.

Pastor Brad Borowski can be found just a state over in the northern part of Nevada. He is a part of the Living Stones Network of churches, which is a group of churches that seek to proclaim truth and the gospel of Christ, a group of people whose lives have been changed by the good news of Jesus and are gathered together to be used by Him to share the message with others. Pastor Brad said it is a family of independent churches that banded together to plant more churches and see a spiritual shift in northern Nevada. Nothing revolutionary, just being the ancient church in modern times.

Nevada is an interesting state. I remember driving through it from Arizona. First, you encounter the excitement and action of Henderson and Las Vegas, which are at the bottom of the state. As you leave these cities, you enter the desert. It seems like it never ends. Heading north, you will pass hundreds of miles of desert, flat desert with hardly any buildings which seems to go forever. I worried about running out of gas because there was no cell phone service or any signs of life outside this cement road through the desert. You finally reach highway I-80, which connects Salt Lake City and Reno, Nevada. You begin to see small towns and signs of life along this highway. And then north of it, you start getting into some of the mountains and beauty that can be found in Idaho.

This is the area where Pastor Brad Borowski can be found. Pastor Brad says that we need to rebuild trust in presenting the gospel message and actually go out and proclaim it. Some Christians have a reputation for being inauthentic, so we need to be authentic.

The church as a whole has done poorly in the last fifty to sixty years and eroded some trust as we have moved to a postmodern culture. Rebuild that trust. It is okay to respond to sharing faults and sins from the pulpit, while not endorsing them, as being real can prevent the legitimacy of doubts. Be authentic to understanding the position of the people as we help them see Christian growth not only about doing more but rather the sin beneath the sin. Trust is built with consistency and comes from integrity. We need authentic gospel-centeredness, not just with works. Do not get legalistic. It is found in grace alone and Christ alone. Be authentic. Do not pretend to be something you are not.

Pastor Brad says that the world needs to see the things we are saying. Do not change. They need to see real-life change. Serve the poor, care for the sick, and do things. Do it authentically because you are so overwhelmed with the grace of God. One problem that we see is the church creating conflict and arguing politics. Some churches go backward or too far forward and get progressive and lose the heart of the gospel or hold on to old methods and traditions a little too tightly. Other churches hold too strongly to old methods and traditions. Ancient creeds and liturgical methods are helpful, but we need to speak in a way that people understand today.

Pastor Brad talks about people finding faith in Christ for the first time, even though they have been to church for a long time. Pastor Brad is able to baptize a lot of people who might have been cultural Christians or former Catholics who were just caught in the religious structure of the system. They had no idea what the gospel message and the key to salvation were, even though they had been to the church for a long time. Some may have been cultural Christians who believed that being a good Christian person was just going to church and being a good person. Others might have been former Catholics who got caught in an ancient church confessional structure of sin and assurance of pardon and got tied into a works-flavored gospel instead of the true gospel.

Many of these people went through the motions, whether this was at a Protestant or Catholic Church. They might have taken the sacraments, sang some songs, or gave some money, but they had no true faith in Christ or even an understanding of what it meant to be saved. They dated the method and married the mission. For some, they might have gotten married or divorced there. Pastor Brad thinks it is important to meet people where they are at. He works with a lot of Hispanics, Catholics, and unchurched groups.

Pastor Brad tells the story of one man in particular who was a Hispanic man. He decided to check out the church along with his wife. They were able to relate to it because some of the language and creeds from the ancient church were used in the service. They said that they went to a church for a long time, but they never really understood what they were saying or doing. They never understood, never believed, though they wanted to believe and wanted to be a real authentic follower of Jesus.

Pastor Brad understands how it is to belong to a church network. He mentions that down in the south, there is a lot of social status that comes along with going to church. Some people go to church because their friends do, and it is more of a social club. Where he is at, there is none of that. Most people do not go to church. Some may go for relationships or the legalistic structure of it, but many do not. He sees it as an opportunity to rescue more people. He also advises not to just leave your church because you like something else better. Go back to your original church and try to help make it better, though he acknowledges that it might be near impossible to change a church unless it is solidly gospel-centered and humble while also being open to being influenced. But you can with the power of God and the Bible as your source of truth.

Today, we have multiple movements infiltrating the church that really have one primary objective which is to take the main message of Christianity, the gospel, the cross, and the atonement, and tuck them away and hide them so that we can bring in secondary issues and make them the primary focus. There are all kinds of good things churches can talk about and focus on—love, self-improvement, declaring victory in your life, being part of something bigger than yourself, how to overcome the enemy and challenges in your life, etc. And these things can all be good things unto themselves. We just have to be careful with taking these secondary issues and making them the primary issue. You cannot have a church without the gospel. You can have a building, have an institution, create legacies, and even help out the community. But without the main point, the cross, the gospel, and Christ crucified, you are missing the point.

But this is not bad news but rather good news. Truth, freedom, and victory can be found on the cross. While we have enough bad news today, the gospel message offers us good news. No longer do we have to be slaves and prisoners to fear, death, and the destructive power of sin but find freedom through the cross.

4

Trapped

According to the CDC,[13] over one million people have died from the coronavirus disease also known as COVID. Many people lost friends, family members, and neighbors. It has impacted people across the globe and altered many lives. Everyone's reaction to COVID was different. Some people locked themselves in their houses with masks on for a few years. Others had a relaxed approach to it, seemingly ignoring it and not letting it impact their daily lives. And governments around the globe reacted differently. Some allowed people to make their own health choices; others decided it for them. So COVID created a few questions. Should we sacrifice our individual liberties for more governmental control for the greater good of the people? Is the government always concerned about the greater good of the people? And most importantly, should the government be involved in the affairs of the church?

The Bible tells us to obey our government. We have "render to Caesar the things that are Caesar's, and to God the things that are God's."[14] Also, "let every person be subject to the governing authorities. For there is no authority except from God, and those that exist have been instituted by God."[15] This verse seems to show us that

---

[13] Centers for Disease Control and Prevention, (n.d.), *CDC Covid Data tracker.* Centers for Disease Control and Prevention, Retrieved February 20, 2023, from https://covid.cdc.gov/covid-data-tracker/#datatracker-home.

[14] Matthew 22:21 (KJV)

[15] Romans 13:1 (ESV)

Christians need to submit and surrender to the governing authorities. Yet the apostles, early church, and numerous Christians throughout history have not done this and have been beaten, tortured, and executed for standing against Governmental authorities. Acts 5:29 says, "We must obey God rather than Man"

At what point does a Christian stand up and resist the government? Did not the early disciples stand up to the Roman government and get executed for it? Have not Christians across the globe been executed for resisting governmental authority? Furthermore, at what point does the church stand up against the culture that is surrounding it? Should the culture be impacting the church, or should the church be impacting the culture?

Up in the western part of Canada, where it stays cold, we can find the province of Alberta. Graced along the edges of the Rocky Mountains, with gorgeous lakes and mountains, we can find some of the most beautiful and incredible scenery this world has to offer. We can also find Pastor Artur Pawlowski of Street Church. While Pastor Pawlowski now resides in Canada, he previously resided in Poland. Sandwiched in the eastern part of Europe, Poland has a history of being subjected to invaders and tyrants. Pastor Pawlowski grew up under socialism. He heard stories from his grandparents, would visit concentration camps as a child, and listened to stories from eyewitnesses about the atrocities Poland faced living under Nazi Germany. What we read about in our history books, Pastor Pawlowski would experience firsthand from stories told by his family, friends, and neighbors. While Pastor Pawlowski now lives in Canada, he carries with him his Polish memories, heritage, and a distinctively Polish accent.

When the COVID crisis started taking away the rights of its Canadian citizens, Pastor Pawlowski knew he could not just sit around and listen to stories, like he did as a child. So when the Canadian government said the homeless people in Canada would no longer be fed due to COVID, Pastor Pawlowski went out in the fresh air and fed them. When Canada said liquor and marijuana were essential but not the church, he held church services. When Canada told him to shut up, he spoke out. Because he went against the government narrative, he was assaulted, arrested, and thrown in solitary confinement.

When asked if what he was doing contrasted Romans 13, the pastor responded that there was no contrast because power, order, and structure come from God. If those who are supposed to protect you are working against you, a decision has to be made if you are going to obey an earthly king or the King of kings. You have to be very careful what law you are willing to follow as God's law supersedes man's law. The one whom you obey becomes the God that you have chosen to worship. He stated that

> No one can serve two masters, for either he
> will hate the one and love the other, or he will
> be devoted to the one and despise the other. You
> cannot serve God and money.[16]

When you obey God, He sets you free; when you obey the devil, he shackles you.

Pastor Pawlowski explained that whether you are dealing with communism, fascism, or any totalitarian regime, you have to deal with the desire of the government to take the place of God, to be a Pharaoh. The things he was told not to do such as worshiping, gathering together, and administering the Lord's supper, you must do. God lives in the praises of His people. There can be no division among you, Romans 2:11, Romans 10:12, and Hebrews 10:24. Jeremiah 20:13 tells us that God is first and always first and anything above is an idol. In the book of Acts in chapter 4, the question is brought up of who we should obey. This is later answered in Acts 5, "We ought to obey God rather than man." We can see an example of a church that obeys God in Acts 2:42,

> And they devoted themselves to the apostles' teaching and the fellowship, to the breaking
> of bread and the prayers.[17]

---

[16] Matthew 6:24 (ESV)

[17] ESV

Pastor Pawlowski is worried that some churches are giving in to fear, not only over this issue but also in everything. Some people feel a need to be terrorized, they are getting caught in bondage and the church is complying. But Pastor Pawlowski also reminds us that while fear is contagious, courage can also be contagious. Pastor Pawlowski is worried that some churches are controlling the people, running things like an operation, and this decline in faith is leading to a great apostasy and falling away. Many churches are selling Jesus for silver, as Judas once did. Ezra sold his birthright for a bowl of soup.

Pastor Pawlowski reminds us that God will not share you with the devil; you have to choose one or the other. Be careful when churches are preaching to the wallet and not to the soul. For some, the focus is not on Christ but on entertainment, healing, supernatural encounters, and focusing on an inward purpose, no desire to carry the cross or encounter any types of suffering. Pastor Pawlowski warns us that we become slaves of whatever we choose to obey. He reminds us about how the Bible warns us about a great falling away, and we might be starting to live in it right now. Speaking as a Canadian with that noticeable Polish accent, Pastor Pawloski concluded the interview with an impassioned charge to "hold the line, because great is the reward when you serve God rather than man."[18]

Control in the church is a theme that is nationwide. External pressures from the government or culture can impact many churches. From traveling, I have met many people hurt, wounded and have been abused by people in power. When asked about this, Pastor Todd Petty from Hillside Church stated that he has seen and experienced it. His concern is that the church in America, and for that matter the pastors in America, have elevated the role of "*the* pastor." So Pastor Todd has been able to focus on getting amateurs, people who do things not because they are getting paid or have a title or position but for the love of God, equipped into different roles in ministry service.

---

[18] The Alberta Court of Appeals ruled in favor of this pastor and ordered Alberta health services to pay him and his brother $15,733.59, though Canada is still fighting him. https://www.christianpost.com/news/pastor-artur-pawlowski-wins-legal-victory-covid-19-orders.html

Pastor Todd's goal has been to decentralize the role of the pastor. When the position of the pastor is elevated, it leads to more powerful positions for the pastor but not necessarily putting the people in the body of Christ in the correct positions.

> Power tends to corrupt and absolute power
> corrupts absolutely.[19]

One problem with putting the pastor at the top is that the top is a lonely place. Too many pastors are alone because they have elevated the position to be *the* pastor, and *the* is a lonely word. So you end up in a situation that is not good for the pastor or the congregation.

Pastor Todd reminds us that the disciples were basically amateurs, mostly fishermen. Yet they turned the world upside down. So Pastor Todd wonders about what would happen if pastors prepared God's people for works of service so that *ministry amateurs* did the work of ministry because they loved Jesus, instead of paid professionals. He says that he has tried to do this, but "it was always a fight." But he works on making disciples, not creating titles and putting people on payroll, as much of this can be done by ministry amateurs. In some cases, he has encouraged people to leave the church and serve elsewhere, as God leads them.

He reminds everyone that we are building a family of disciples, not trying to grow a church. That is God's job. Work with whoever you have, release them for ministry, and use that as training. Making disciples involves training ministry amateurs, not hiring paid professionals. Decentralize the role of the pastor, raise up other leaders, and allow them to develop a team of others who are serving alongside ministry amateurs. He states that Ephesians 4:16 still works:

> From whom the whole body, joined and held
> together by every joint with which it is equipped,

---

[19] Quote attributed to the nineteenth-century English historian Lord Acton (1834–1902) in a letter to Bishop Mandell Creighton about how historians should judge the abuse of power by past rulers, especially popes.

when each part is working properly, makes the
body grow so that it builds itself up in love.[20]

He also reminds us that taking a day off is mandatory as it proves to everyone including yourself that you believe in God, He is able, He is enough, He said to do it, and when we do it, it proves that He is. The work will never be done, and no matter how much you do, someone will notice what you did not do and point it out. Just because you learned something in Bible college does not mean to stop being a student of His word. Finally, keep a humble heart before the Lord.

Trust in the Lord with all thine heart; and
lean not unto thine own understanding. In all
thy ways acknowledge him, and he shall direct
thy paths.[21]

Control in the church is really found in three different areas. We have external control that comes from the government. We recently saw this a lot in Canada and to a lesser extent in America. We also have cultural control. There was a time when the church would influence the culture. You can see this in poetry, art, and music with Bach, Michelangelo, Leonardo da Vinci, and others. Today, in some areas, the culture is controlling the church.

The third type of control that we have is internal control, control that comes from within the church. Sometimes pastors take a leadership role that is stronger than it should be. People are not put into positions that they want to use to glorify God if they are not on the good side of the pastor. Likewise, they will get removed from those positions if they do not agree with everything he says. This can become unhealthy. Some church services are designed to stroke the ego of the pastor or those in leadership. In many cases, other speakers are brought in to speak, but in some cases, they are just there to

---

[20] ESV

[21] Proverbs 3:5–6 (KJV)

remind the audience how great the pastor is. In some cases, this can even manifest itself to become cult-like or even become a cult.

Sometimes churches exhibit more control than they should. Freedom in Christ Jesus can sometimes take a backseat to the power of the institution. What is best for the people might not be as important as what is best for the institution. And the thirst for status and recognition from the leaders can take precedence over what is best for the body of Christ.

Control is something that is not recognizable at first. It sneaks in, is subtle, and happens slowly over time. It starts with little things, control over the direction of a program, control over who is getting hired, control with the direction of the church. But it can end when the tentacles of control are firmly entwined in a believer's mind. Instead of finding freedom in life under our Father in heaven, they find they are tied to control, fear, and the bondage of the institution. Maybe they questioned how a pastor's teaching did not align with the Bible and were rebuked for it. Maybe they tried out for a ministry but were rejected not due to personal qualifications but due to their loyalty to leadership. Maybe they missed some religious meetings or did not praise the greatness of the pastor enthusiastically enough. These people cannot truly experience the freedoms that can be found in Christ Jesus until they are freed from the institution that is holding them in bondage.

If a church does have a problem with control, it will oftentimes go unnoticed until you have been around for a while. In many cases, it ends with the pastor's words taking precedence over the Word of God. It can sometimes end in a cult. The word *cult* sounds scary and oftentimes conjures up images of Hollywood movies and people drinking goat's blood, David Koresh, Jim Jones, or Marshall Applewhite. And there are cults like this. But for the most part, a cult is a group of people whose teachings or beliefs are different from mainstream historical traditional Christianity. Their views are going to differ slightly from the mainstream historical church. So we are dealing with a theological cult with a social/psychological bent.

Jesus Christ is the head of the church. Principles of the faith have been established through doctrines, creeds, and covenants and cemented by leaders, the disciples, Polycarp, Spurgeon, Wesley, Whitefield, Luther, etc. When you start moving toward a cult, there is going to be some doctrine, some idea, or some belief that contradicts historical, biblical, traditional, and orthodox Christianity, some kind of greater revelation that was not there before. The people will now look to the leader before they look to God. They will now look to the writings provided by this group before they look to the Holy Bible. They will look to the special revelation of the group, before any revelation that we have in the Bible. In some cases, this control can manifest itself in such a way that it forms into a cult or cult-like attributes.

In 610 AD, amid an area stepped in pagan worship, we have a man who started having visions in a cave. He was originally worried that "possession of the devil which I feared all along" had come to pass but later attributed these visions to the angel Gabriel. His revelations were written down in a book, and he claimed to be a prophet, along the lines of Abraham, Moses, Isaiah, Daniel, and Jesus, just another prophet among others. He took these prophecies to his friends and neighbors, fellow Jews, remnants from the Babylonian captivity, and later Persian control. This man, Mohammad, introduced himself to his Jewish neighbors as another prophet. But they rightfully rejected him, as most of them have rejected the true prophet. So Mohammad pushed his religion by the blade of the sword, and the Jews they lived among would never again be called friends and neighbors.

Islam and Mohammad are an extreme example, and not a cult of Christianity but rather its own religion. But it gives us warning signs, when someone declares themselves to be a prophet and provides their own writings to replace or supplement the Bible, we are going to have a problem. Islam is just an example of an extreme problem. The Mormon church has a president and an appointed quorum of twelve Apostles that get direct revelation from God and then give it to the common man. There is structure and control in place. The president and apostles set the rules, hear from God, then give it to the church goers, as they cannot hear from God themselves. Mormons are given *The Book of Mormon*, as a sacred text along with the *Doctrine and Covenants* and the *Pearl of Great Price*. The Mormons acknowledge the actual Bible but use a heavily cross-referenced version of it. Since the Bible has two testaments, they see *The Book of Mormon* as the third testament of Jesus Christ.

Jehovah's Witnesses do not see Jesus as having any divinity but rather see him as a creation of God. Instead of the Bible, they rely on their distorted watchtower tracks as their primary path to truth. They have created their own version of the Bible, the *New World Translation* or NWT. The NWT changed the original scriptures to twist and align themselves with the beliefs of the Jehovah's Witnesses and was created with "no known translators with recognized degrees in Greek or Hebrew exegesis or translation."[22] The founder of the religion, Charles Taze Russell, "once declared that it would be better to leave the Scriptures unread and read his books rather than to read the Scriptures and neglect his books."[23] This is the reason that they do not leave your doorstep after you tell them you are a Christian. They are not looking to pull you to Christ but pull you into their organization.

Christian Science was started by Mary Baker Eddy; they believe that sickness is an illusion that can be handled by prayer only. And prayer does conquer sickness, the problem is you do not need to rely on the teachings of Mary Baker Eddy and be under their writings, doctrines, and sets of rules. You can access God and healing on your own. Like all distortions of Christianity, Christian scientists alter the truth and deny that Jesus is God and believe that sin, death, and evil do not exist, and rely on their own writings instead of the Word of God.

There are numerous other cults, schisms, and divisions in Christianity, too many to mention. What we can see in all of them is a pattern. It starts with control in the church. Control in the church starts with the leader wanting to put his ideas and methods in front of God's ways. Really it is a way for them to feel powerful; they are taking away some of the thunder from God. Instead of looking to

---

[22] Martin, Walter, and Ravi K. Zacharias. *The Kingdom of the Cults* (Minneapolis, MN: Bethany House Publishers, 2003), 93.

[23] Martin, Walter, and Ravi K. Zacharias, *The Kingdom of the Cults* (Minneapolis, MN: Bethany House Publishers, 2003), 57.

the Creator, you look to the pastor or leader. Control in the church leads to an unhealthy church. Unhealthy churches can sometimes become so unhealthy that they pick up cult-like attributes or become a cult. There are really three main characteristics that you can find in an unhealthy church that exhibits control in a type of theological or psychological cult.

1. They will change the definition of atonement. Instead of declaring that salvation comes through faith in Christ Jesus and His atonement on the cross as salvation for your sins, they will declare another way for salvation. Generally, this way of salvation can only be found through them.
2. They will not follow a traditional Bible but will bring in supplemental writings that they see as being equal to the Bible or intentionally change the Bible.
3. They are going to elevate their leader, either as a person with wisdom and spiritual guidance above the common person or in more extreme cases as a prophet or apostle equal to or above the levels of the prophets in the Bible. They will claim additional revelation from God through dreams, visions, or anointed wisdom directly from God.

Pastor Ryan Glosson runs the First Baptist Church in Turbeville South Carolina. Some of these small towns in the deep south are neat. I had the opportunity to live in the small town next to it for a period. You could have one grocery store, one post office, one school, one gas station, and seven churches. This town is only slightly bigger and has twelve churches. Southern hospitality is still a real thing; people are just nicer down here and take more time to great each other. Sweet tea flows like water and things slow down just a little bit in the hot summer. Neighbors are also friends and strangers are neighbors. There seems to be less hostility and animosity toward each other than you see in the states north of them; maybe it is because they are cold and grumpy half the year.

Pastor Ryan understands how control works because he grew up in it. His church started off doing all the right things. Solid preaching and a commitment to following the Bible and all the commandments in the Bible. And that is a good thing and the desire to do that likely comes from a pure heart. You do want to honor God and follow His commandments. The opposite extreme is using grace as a free for license to sin, and not following any of God's commandments and living in a perpetual state of rebellion. So the church Pastor Ryan was involved in was following God's commandments. But then they started adding a few rules of their own, just to make sure. Then they added some more rules and some more rules. The rules became so plenteous that they started adding in some rules just to make sure that you were following all the rules. It went into legalism and then beyond legalism.

Since many of these rules were not in the Bible, you had to be in this little group to really know the rules. Or how else would you know that you could not wear wire-rimmed glasses because the Beatles wore wire-rimmed glasses? How else would you know how to cut your hair or what clothing was okay to wear? There were boxes to check. And then when everyone was able to check all those boxes, some more rules were added. And then some more rules. And then some more rules.

Then you needed a leader to enforce all the biblical rules, non-biblical rules, and extra-biblical rules. And this leader needed authority, or how else would you figure out who could belong to the group and who God hated or if more new rules needed to be added? And it was an unwritten and well-known rule to never challenge the leader; that was the golden rule. And the leader controlled and dictated people's lives. But there were advantages. Once you were solidly into this little group, you were able to start looking disapprovingly toward other people who were not in your little group. And then some anger starts sneaking in. And then before you know it, without signing up for it, control has a grip on your life. And you see everything from a judgmental point of view and an angry point of view. And then you start controlling those around you and in your family.

One thing that Pastor Ryan said that really stuck out is that even if another group checked all the boxes, even if another group followed all the biblical rules and extra-biblical rules and made-up rules right down to a T, you still could not associate with them. They were bad. Everyone outside his little Independent Fundamental Baptist group was bad. If you believed that the King James Version of the Bible was the only reliable version of the Bible, and everyone that reads a different version is bad, this group took it a step further and said that the 1611 version of the KJV is the only version of the Bible that you can read. But even if you only faithfully read the 1611 KJV,[24] vowed to never wear wire-rimmed glasses, listen to the Beatles, play cards, or dance or have any fun whatsoever, if you were in a different Independent Fundamental Baptist group, you were still somehow the enemy, even if you agreed on the exact same things. And all agreed to never have any fun.

Pastor Ryan Glosson reminds us that it is not about making a bunch of rules to follow and that there is really one essential rule that we need to follow, and that is blasphemy of the Holy Spirit. It is not about doing religious things but about a relationship, that we do not need all these extra-biblical rules; we just need to follow the commands listed in scripture.

> The church does not help when it claims
> God says when he does not, or that God does not
> say when he does.[25]

One dangerous thing that Pastor Ryan has seen is that this cult-like control is weaving its way into mainstream churches. They might not be cults, but the leader is acting like they are. Some leaders are making sure that those who are in power in the church align with their views, including elders and deacons. The real danger is when you cannot question leadership, or you will be ostracized from the organization. When the Man of God narrative gets too strong, it

---

[24] Pastor Ryan says that the KJV is still his favorite translation, and this is not an attack on this translation, but rather an attack on the idea that this is the only translation available in the church today for English-speaking people or that salvation is somehow only found through this translation. Pastor Ryan currently uses the ESV for his congregation.

[25] Pastor Ross Shannon First Baptist Church of Lapeer

can get dangerous. If you have to work your way into the *in crowd*, and the pastor is above reproach, it is a problem. If the pastor loses control and starts kicking people out over personal issues, it is problematic. Many times, these people stop building Christ's kingdom, and it becomes about building their own personal institution.

One solution Pastor Ryan sees is showing love. Love needs to be the glue that holds the church together. He said millennials in particular are relational. Beware of soft theology that is a mile wide and an inch deep. He reminds us that we do not need to fight over small trivial issues but fight for the essentials, the trinity, death, burial, and resurrection. If God protected Adam in the Garden from the tree of life, He is going to protect us. The Word of God is sufficient; we do not need extra-biblical rules. He does not want sacrifices; He wants you. While God does get jealous and angry, He is ultimately a God of love. He loves you.

5

The Lucrative Message

Out in the Texas desert heat, the speaker commanded the stage. A polished speaker with years of experience, he attracted a large audience. While only a few thousand may fill the church, the audience who listens online or divulges in some other form of communication is worldwide. Speaking with a Southern drawl, animated gestures, and an excited voice, his eyes almost popped out with enthusiasm as his hands pierced the air. The crowd was captivated by every word, and a nervous excitement filled the room. Promises were made by the man on the stage, and dreams and ideas started dancing through the audience members' heads. What if what he was saying was true? Could this be real? If they could just live the life that the speaker was talking about, how much better things would be for them?

The audience was filled with members in pain. Those with various types of cancers, diabetes, head injuries, aches, pains, and ailments. They started envisioning themselves with a life free of all these types of symptoms. Those who were sitting in wheelchairs started picturing themselves walking free out of the chair, out in the sun, among the flowers, and the trees, the sun on their face, and the wind in their hair. How good it would feel to stop the chemotherapy treatments, how good it would feel to be able to sleep at night, how good it would feel to be able to walk again.

Others were relatively healthy; they were not even there for themselves; they were there for their children, their parents, or their loved ones. They had problems, serious problems, and they were desperate for a solution. They needed answers. The doctors were not providing hope, the hospitals were not providing hope, and their medication was not providing hope. But this man was. He said if you would just give him some money, just keep giving him money, but do it in faith, all your problems would be solved. The cancers would dissipate, the backs would be healed, and the vision would be restored; all it would take was a little bit of money.

Others were there for a different reason. They were healthy. But some were under crushing financial bondages. Some were under burdens of debt. Others were not in debt, but they wanted more; no, they needed more. The more the speaker talked, the more the images of lust bounced around in their head. The man on stage had no problem with greed; in fact, he endorsed it. He was prideful of all that he had and he planned to get more. Almost a billionaire with multiple jets, cars, and houses, he flaunted and bragged about his wealth, wealth that would come from those in the audience. All they had to do was give him some of their money, and that wealth would belong to them also.

Visions of better cars, better houses, better jobs, and a better life started dancing around in the audience members' heads. It could all belong to them. And all they had to do was give this man a little bit of their money and believe in faith, and they could have whatever they wanted. As prompted, some started shouting out what they wanted and declaring it in this life—cars, houses, vacations, healings, prosperity. They felt emboldened and encouraged by this man who referred to himself as a preacher, and they wanted what he had.

Some people claim that these speakers are God's anointed prophets and get messages directly from God himself. Others claim that what he is pushing has nothing to do with God and more to do with his Greed. What is the truth? And does it matter?

There are certain keywords, phrases, lingos, and terms that are unique to those in the prosperity gospel circles. There are a few hand-picked scriptures that are memorized and quoted frequently. The theology works best by hammering these verses into memory and repeatedly saying these phrases over and over again. It does not work very well if you start going through the entire Bible and try some type of expository preaching style. For this to work, you need to craft more stories and examples, from your personal life or the Bible and hammer the people with these select verses throughout the sermon. Sermons are crafted more to push their theology than push what the Bible has to say.

Oftentimes, you can walk into any prosperity gospel-focused church and recognize the focus of the church from just one sermon, as these select phrases and terms will be continually presented. By handpicking these phrases and verses, a new version of the Bible can be presented, one that is more suited for an American, capitalistic, and materialistic society.

But like everything America does, it is now getting exported across the globe. Adherents of the prosperity gospel generally are not told that they are signing up to be a part of the prosperity gospel. This has no denominational barrier line; it crosses denominational lines. While many churches in different denominations will outright reject prosperity theology, other churches will embrace it. So what are these terms? What are the phrases?

We have the seed faith theory, the idea that we give money to a person, and then God will give us more money back. But it has to be done out of faith, or else you really do not get anything back, also known as the give-to-get theory. You give money, and God gives you extra money back. Kind of like a bank or the stock market. Many times, it is also referred to as your seed. Your *seed* refers to the money that you give. You sow it, water it, and nurture it with faith, and God gives you money back. It is a neat concept; it just has no bearing on reality or the Bible. Oftentimes promises are made and tied into the seed faith theory. That if you give to them, God will give you more money back. They manipulate Mark 4:8 as the foundational verse:

> Still other seed fell on good soil. It came
> up, grew and produced a crop, some multiplying
> thirty, some sixty, some a hundred times.[26]

---

[26] Mark 4:8 (NIV)

So the claim made by some is that if you give them money, you get a hundred times back. But this shows the danger of manipulating a verse out of context. Jesus is giving a parable here, and He explains His parable just a few verses later; He is talking about the word.

> The farmer sows the word. Some people are like seed along the path, where the word is sown. As soon as they hear it, Satan comes and takes away the word that was sown in them. Others, like seed sown on rocky places, hear the word and at once receive it with joy. But since they have no root, they last only a short time…Others, like seed sown on good soil, hear the word, accept it, and produce a crop—some thirty, some sixty, some a hundred times what was sown.[27] (Mark 4:14–20)

We have the Abrahamic covenant, where we branch into all the Abrahamic blessings. Name it and claim it or positive confession gets talked about a lot. God will give us whatever we want, as long as we declare what we want and claim it for ourselves. In many circles, it is okay if you do not even have any money, just send some out of faith anyways, borrow it, or use your credit card, and this will lead to supernatural debt cancellation. In some circles, the atonement is so far twisted to such an extent that they are claiming that Jesus Christ did not die on the cross for your sins but rather for your financial gain.

In many of these churches, the services are all geared up and structured to focus on the main event, offering time. The pastor starts speaking with a fervent passion, the music starts getting faster and more exciting, promises are made, and declarations are declared. It is time to give now, and this giving will change your life. One church plays a song: Money, money, come to me, fly to me on wings of eagles—as congregants shout out declarations of what they want. But who are you really giving to? Are you really giving to God, or is it more the guy on stage?

---

[27] Portion comes from Mark 4:14–20 (NIV)

Pastor Henry Bechthold was a pastor in Minnesota for twenty-five years; he now helps run an inner-city outreach and teaches, writes books, and speaks. Apparently along with an enjoyment for being cold most of the year, he enjoys speaking and writing on some of the issues that are prevalent in the church today. One of the things that he speaks against is the prosperity gospel. The main problem that Pastor Henry sees with the prosperity gospel is that it is not the real gospel. While the real gospel will encourage us to engage in active outreach and help the poor, needy, and the homeless, the prosperity gospel encourages us to be inward focused.

Pastor Henry reminds us that we need to be outward focused because we have a sin problem in the church and the church does not want to talk about theological issues and presses back against those who want to lead the church to righteousness. Pastor Henry says that this reminds him that Jesus was not only tortured but also humiliated. Sometimes standing for the truth will lead to humiliation and put you on a difficult path, and you need to be careful because the goats are feeding among the sheep.

Pastor Henry once did some calculations on all the income that prosperity preachers brought in across America. And he said that instead of these preachers spending the money on themselves for houses, yachts, jets, and mansions, if this money was equally distributed across America, it could house, feed, and clothe every single homeless person in the United States of America. Pastor Henry says that the greatest danger that we see in the church today is silence. Silence about church, silence about false teachings, and silence about truth. We need Jesus as the Savior but also as Lord.

Do not hold on to sin; if we do hold on to sin, Jesus will not hear us. He warns us to not be silent. The silence will grieve us. Men of God need to stand up and preach in the church. Leaders especially cannot be silent and need to stand up for righteousness and truth. Get into the Bibles and get the truth out of them. Do not listen to a give-to-get philosophy. We are supposed to give to serve others. And most importantly, we need to invade the world instead of allowing the world to invade the church.

The idea that you have to financially pay to earn God's favor is not necessarily a new one. Antiquity shows us countless examples of men offering up various sacrifices to various gods for health, favor, or protection. Pope Urban II first offered indulgences back in 1095 during the crusades where he remitted penance to everyone who participated in the crusades and confessed their sins. Indulgences were also offered to those who could not go on the Crusades but were offered cash contributions. By the time Martin Luther reached the scene in the sixteenth century, the wealth of the Roman Catholic Church was unprecedented; they controlled as much and had as much wealth as some of the great empires of world history. Everything in the Catholic Church was for sale, positions in the church were bought, peasants had to pay for a child to be baptized, and peasants paid for each service, on top of their tithes and working the church land. On top of these other fees, the Catholic Church used the indulgence system.

Indulgences were certificates that you could purchase to cover past and current sins. They had all kinds of indulgences and point systems to cover your sins and guarantee your salvation. You even had an obligation to purchase indulgences for dead family members and relatives so they could get out of purgatory in case they were not able to purchase enough indulgences during their time on this earth. Indulgences could even be purchased for future sins that were about to be committed. In one interesting scenario, a man purchased indulgences to cover his future sin of robbing the man who was selling indulgences.[28]

To give the Catholic Church credit, they have mostly abandoned the indulgence system. But some of the Protestants have repackaged it. This time around, you are not purchasing for eternity, but purchasing for *favor* and *anointing*, for right now. Old ideas have been repackaged into new methodologies to gain wealth for a few. In Luther's day, religious figures would tell you that you needed to pay money to atone for your sins to keep your salvation. Today, you are told that you need to pay money to have God's favor and anointing in this life.

---

[28] Eric Metaxas, *Martin Luther: The Man Who Rediscovered God and Changed the World*. (New York: Penguin Books, 2018), 106.

As this life takes precedence over eternal life, a lack of giving and faith is always the response to a lack of money or healing. Under true prosperity theology, if you speak against these "men of God," you will be cursed and lose God's blessing. But if you give enough money, you will be healthy, wealthy, and prosperous. Today we are no longer buying indulgences but buying anointing, favors, and blessings in this life for right now. This medieval system has been repackaged for modern-day America.

Pastor John Glenn runs Amazing Grace Baptist Church on the windward-swept side of the Southern end of the Big Island of Hawaii. It might be one of the best spots on the island. You can go to a black sand beach and swim with the sea turtles, try a green sand beach if that is more your thing, or just stick with a normal golden sand beach. If you are adventures, just skip the beaches and jump off a cliff into the ocean. You can find a lot of wild tropical fruit trees in this area if you know where to look. They also have some good orchards and coffee farms. It is here where you can find Pastor John. He preaches out of a large tent that they pop up on Sunday. I first met Pastor John years before writing this book. He gave a powerful sermon on the dangers of the prosperity gospel and why this had no place in the church and warned about the major characters that were involved in it, so I knew he had to be in the book. Pastor John used to live in Italy, before moving to the mountains of Hawaii.

Pastor John was asked a few common questions regarding the prosperity gospel. The first one gets played out a lot in churches across America every Sunday, sometimes subtly, sometimes blatantly. And that was if God curses or blesses people based on their giving to the church. Pastor John responded with a story that he was once ministering in a church in Italy. After the message, one of the brothers came up to ask him a question. He wanted to know if it was okay for a pastor to tell one of the church members that it was okay to make money in drug trafficking as long as you gave some of that money to the church. Pastor John thought he was joking at first but then realized that he was not joking. He had to come to terms with the reality that there were people out there calling themselves pastors of Christ's sheep and were teaching them such deception.

Pastor John said that God, who owns the cattle on a thousand hills and creates the heaven and the earth for His pleasure and our good, does not need anything of material value from man. It is actually a curse upon that individual that proclaims that people are blessed or cursed based solely on material giving or the lack thereof. It is simply deception for those who *claim* to be sons of God to manipulate people by twisting the Scripture because of their love of money.

The Lord has always looked at the heart. It is the heart of faith that pleases the Lord as we see in Hebrews 11:6. This is the real economy of God, not the might, wealth, or wisdom of mankind but the faith of mankind in their Creator.

No wonder the poor widow could give so little in monetary value, and yet it be esteemed the greater amount in comparison to all the rich religious elites who could give so much more, and yet it be esteemed so little by Christ. Giving will always be based on the righteous standard of Christ. He searches the heart. He will know which are like the poor widow and those who are like Ananias and Sapphira, and even those that tithe of all they possess, and yet they are unrighteous before God in their heart. (Luke 18:12)

Pastor John was then asked if Jesus and the apostles were rich as this is a claim made by some prosperity pastors. He responded that we do not know for certain how rich or poor the disciples really were. We know that some of the disciples like Matthew had jobs that probably allowed them to support themselves quite well. But when the Son of Man came, their lives on earth would never be the same.

Matthew 19:27 certainly gives us some insight. It is clear from the words of Peter that they were not getting hundredfold material blessings. It is unlikely they were sporting fancy homes and traveling in horse-drawn chariots. They had left everything in this present material existence to follow Christ. Christ left the highest position in existence to come to earth. It is said in Matthew 8:20,

> The Son of Man hath no place to lay His
> head.

The riches that Christ sought were captive souls that needed to be redeemed (Luke 19:10). The disciples embraced this, and they took up their crosses and followed Him. The very idea that they took up their *cross* and followed Him speaks volumes.

Pastor John then addressed how prosperity gospel preachers present poor people as either people who have not quite yet figured out God's blessing system or to the more extreme extent that they are cursed and hated by God. Pastor John responded that it is jaw-dropping to think that one who is a sinner yet claims to be a child of the Highest by the grace and finished work of Jesus Christ that this individual would turn and speak to the poor as if they are hated or cursed by God. He said he was reminded of the passage in Matthew 19:21 when the rich man came to Christ and claimed that he was stellar in his obedience to God. He asked Jesus what was lacking. The Lord told him to give up all his riches and not just give them up but give them to the poor.

The man could not do it. Wow! Pastor John said that it always amazes him that there are those people who claim to know the Savior but will gladly take money from the poor, but they will not give anything to the poor (1 John 3:16–18). This is not just being under-shepherded; they are not worthy to be serving in places of leadership in the Lord's church. First Timothy 3 makes it clear that no deacon or bishop should be greedy of filthy lucre. No Christian should be greedy for filthy lucre or dishonest financial gain.

Pastor Artur Pawlowski out of Canada reminds us that God is a giver of wealth; He has no problem with the idea of wealth. But He reminds us that Paul was naked, hungry, and shipwrecked and spent half of a chapter talking about this. Did he sin against God? Pastor Art reminds us that the list of those who had to pay a terrible price to follow the God of the Bible is extensive. God can give you great wealth and riches to use for great purposes; He did for David. But God also allows poverty. Look at Job. Sometimes challenging circumstances are necessary; look at Paul. To suggest otherwise is simply heresy. Pastor Art asks us this: If you have great wealth or any type of wealth, do you hoard it or send it to the kingdom of God?

One extreme that we have seen for those who have rejected the prosperity gospel is that people have the tendency to overcorrect and run in the opposite direction. Pastor Troy Edwards talks about this. He can be found in the tiny state of Rhode Island where he is the pastor of a church and is also the author of multiple books. He tells us: "My perspective on the 'prosperity gospel' as being wrong can be summarized by this one statement by Jesus in Matthew 6:33: 'But seek ye first the kingdom of God, and his righteousness; and all these things shall be added unto you.'" While Jesus promised that God would take care of our material needs (vv. 24–32), He wants our focus to be on the kingdom. Pastor Edwards teaches that God will abundantly take care of our material needs (God is never stingy. He overwhelmingly supplies[Psalm 23]), but a whole ministry should not be centered around teaching this alone at the exclusion of the kingdom of God and its righteousness:

> For the kingdom of God is not meat and
> drink; but righteousness, and peace, and joy in
> the Holy Ghost.[29]

An overemphasis on money causes people to focus more on how to get rich for the sake of getting nice houses, new cars, and other bragging rights and less on how to win souls, support missions, help the poor and hurting, have intercessory prayer, etc. When the focus becomes "What can God do for *me*" rather than "What can I do for God and the furtherance of His kingdom agenda," then we have lost the balance. If getting rich becomes about us then we become no better than that rich man who refused to help poor Lazarus. We all know what happened to him in the end.

Money is addressed throughout the Bible. In the Old Testament, we have stories of Abraham, David, and Solomon. In the Old Testament, righteousness was equated with wealth. The lone exception would really be Job who lost everything even though he was still

---

[29] Romans 14:17 (ESV)

righteous but later got everything back and then some. You have a few verses that allude to this such as:

> This Book of the Law shall not depart from your mouth, but you shall meditate on it day and night, so that you may be careful to do according to all that is written in it. For then you will make your way prosperous, and then you will have good success.[30]

> Blessed is he that considereth the poor: the Lord will deliver him in time of trouble. The Lord will preserve him, and keep him alive; and he shall be blessed upon the earth: and thou wilt not deliver him unto the will of his enemies.[31]

> If you walk in my statutes, and keep my commandments, and do them: Then I will give you rain in due season, and the land shall yield her increase, and the trees of the field shall yield their fruit.[32]

It is important to note that none of these scriptures referring to wealth have anything to do with giving money away to people on the TV set. They do not even involve giving money away but have to deal with righteousness and following God's commandments. But while the Old Testament is our foundation, things changed with the New Testament. There are warnings about wealth. We have John the Baptist who consisted of locusts and wild honey, Jesus who was tortured and killed with no place to lay His head, and all the disciples who also wandered and were all martyred except for John who was

---

[30] Joshua 1:8 (ESV)
[31] Psalm 41:1–2 (KJV)
[32] Leviticus 26:3 (KJV)

exiled on Patmos. From all appearances, they were not living their best life now in some type of Osteenian utopia.

In the New Testament, we learn that instead of equating righteousness with financial blessings, we are implored to give them up. We are also told that God provides, and we do not have to worry about food, eating, and drinking. But we are also reminded that if you do not work you do not eat.[33] So there seems to be a balance. While money itself may be spiritually neutral, the love of money is the root of all evil. We are reminded:

> Not that I am speaking of being in need, for I have learned in whatever situation I am to be content. I know how to be brought low, and I know how to abound. In any and every circumstance, I have learned the secret of facing plenty and hunger, abundance and need. I can do all things through him who strengthens me.[34]

When you put all the pieces of these verses together, it seems that money should not be our primary objective, the kingdom of God should be. God does bless and provide for His children, but the primary objective of our Christian life is not about chasing these blessings but rather chasing after him.

---

[33] 2 Thessalonians 3:10

[34] Philippians 4:11–13 (ESV)

6

A New Excitement

Pastor Leo Robinson II started his multiethnic multicultural church, called Good Church, right in the center of 48505. This zip code is one of the most impoverished areas in America with a medium house value of $31,800 and an average family income of $21,559. Since multiple people and sometimes multiple generations of families oftentimes live in one house, the $21,559 is for the entire family. This is extreme poverty. The unchurched in the area is around 78 percent. Flint Michigan made national news a few years back for the water crisis. Before making national news, people lived with the water situation for half of a decade. Water would come out of the faucets in all different colors. This resulted in skin rashes, teeth would fall out, skin would change color, and hair would fall out from using the water.[35] This is an area where a lot of people do not own their own house, do not own a car, and do not have access to a lot of things available to those in most parts of America. It is a different world.

It is this environment that Pastor Robinson works in. When he hears gunshots, he protects his family and then runs to help the victims. He ministers to crack dealers. Many people see the crack dealers as bad people and a plaque to the community. But Pastor Leo sees

---

[35] "Still Standing: Flint Residents Tell Their Stories about Living with Poisoned Water," Michigan Live, last modified July 1, 2023, https://www.mlive.com/news/page/still_standing_flint_residents.html.

them as just people, people caught in a traumatic situation who do not know any better and are just trying to get by. He recognizes that they really are pillars in the community. People congregate around their front porches. Even police presence does not stop these visits. Pastor Leo recognizes that if he can just impact one crack dealer, or change one life, the influence that this man will now have will impact and change the community. He can reach people that the pastor can never reach. And instead of slinging crack, the former dealer will now be slinging the Good News of the gospel of Jesus Christ.

One point that Pastor Leo brings up is that oftentimes when someone privileged comes into a situation to help out the unprivileged, there is sometimes a subconscious superiority mentality to it. Pastor Leo wonders what it would look like if we were all doing this together, as one, with no superiority. Pastor Leo sees it as what this one person has that the body of Christ does not have. What are they bringing to the body of Christ? What is missing? The people he encounters and works with in Flint have resilience, endurance, strength, an ability to overcome, and patience. They are strong people who have survived and have made it, even without water, food, money, and other things you see throughout traditional America.

Good Church comes from Galatians 6:9–10, that says:

> And let us not grow weary of doing good,
> for in due season we will reap, if we do not give
> up. So then, as we have opportunity, let us do
> good to everyone, and especially to those who are
> of the household of faith.[36]

Good Laundry came out of the church. This was a low-cost program to fight hygiene poverty, which means people do not have access to clean clothes which hinders them from going to work, school, or social functions. Being stinky can be embarrassing. He also leads the members to run Bible studies in coffee shops, houses,

---

[36] ESV

or the local college campus. This brings in a whole new dynamic of people, some of whom never even step foot into the main church. Good Church opened earlier than it originally anticipated; it opened during the COVID crisis. Pastor Leo opened earlier than planned because all the neighboring churches were closed, and there was a group of formerly secular people who were looking for answers to what was happening around them.

One thing Pastor Leo is concerned about is emotionalism. He worries that in some places, emotionalism has consumed the church, to a point that no one is really worried about what the Bible is really saying. If I feel emotion, it has to be good. Some churches are moving to worship-only services that do not even have any preaching or Bible reading. And this is losing a lot of men because men oftentimes do not connect with emotionalism. The Bible is becoming less and less important as everything becomes about feelings. God's word as a foundation gets replaced by how you feel on this particular day. An overcompensation happens as the pastor becomes the man, the center of attention, the person to lead us, oftentimes in the place of God. Instead of relying on the Bible as the Word of God, we rely on the pastor to get a word or message from God.

This puts a lot more pressure on him, more pressure than there should be. And 99 out of 100 times he fails. Or eventually, they will fail 100 percent of the time. Pastor Leo reminds us that we need to bring up strong men and women, and we do this by putting the Bible as our foundation. God's word does this as it cuts and divides truth from error. Songs alone cannot do this; they just guide us along on our emotions.

The emotionalism movement reminds Pastor Leo of his recent reading of Deuteronomy 28. He has heard the verses read, shared, and talked about. And everyone likes these verses, and they are reaffirming. Here they are:

> And if you faithfully obey the voice of the
> Lord your God, being careful to do all his com-
> mandments that I command you today, the Lord
> your God will set you high above all the nations

of the earth. And all these blessings shall come upon you and overtake you, if you obey the voice of the Lord your God. Blessed shall you be in the city, and blessed shall you be in the field. Blessed shall be the fruit of your womb and the fruit of your ground and the fruit of your cattle, the increase of your herds and the young of your flock. Blessed shall be your basket and your kneading bowl. Blessed shall you be when you come in, and blessed shall you be when you go out.[37]

This makes people feel good; it plays to their emotions. Pastor Leo reminds us that nobody wants to read the second half of the chapter; it is as if it does not exist because it does not appeal to our emotions and makes us feel happy. But it is in the exact same chapter, but no one reads it. Here it is:

But if you will not obey the voice of the Lord your God or be careful to do all his commandments and his statutes that I command you today, then all these curses shall come upon you and overtake you. Cursed shall you be in the city, and cursed shall you be in the field. Cursed shall be your basket and your kneading bowl. Cursed shall be the fruit of your womb and the fruit of your ground, the increase of your herds and the young of your flock. Cursed shall you be when you come in, and cursed shall you be when you go out.[38]

It is now understandable why the rest of the chapter does not get read in services, put on coffee mugs, or posted to social media

---

[37] Deuteronomy 28:1–6 (ESV)
[38] Deuteronomy 28:15–20 (ESV)

accounts. But it makes you wonder how many people know that it is there. And it makes you wonder what happens when you ignore part of the Bible and just focus on a few verses that draw on your emotions. And what happens when you neglect the Bible, doctrine, and theology to focus on revelations, feelings, and emotions?

Emotions are a good thing; they are clearly listed in the Bible. David encountered a wide range of emotions, and they are partially recorded in Psalms. Emotions themselves are not problematic. But what is problematic when we allow these emotions to take precedence over the Bible? Today in some churches, we are seeing emotions trump logic, feelings taking precedence over reason, and experiences becoming predominant in the Bible.

This group does not really have an official name. As you can see, bits and pieces of it are in churches across America. There is no denomination or universal covering or official leader. It is mostly just a loose coalition of bits and pieces of theology and ideas that can be found in a variety of churches. One group that is putting together a more streamlined approach to this is the NAR or New Apostolic Reformation. You cannot run a Google search and decide to go to a NAR church even if you wanted to; they do not label themselves as such, so you just kind of stumble upon them. The movement picks up churches that were formerly associated with Pentecostal or Charismatic movements but have diverged from traditional Pentecostal and Charismatic theology. The NAR is starting its own movement that is drifting away from traditional Pentecostal/Charismatic Christianity and also drifting away from traditional biblical Christianity.

Some of the most common NAR beliefs are that the church is going to take dominion of the earth prior to Christ's return[39] and become an aggressive militant army that conquers the Earth.[40] Strategic-level spiritual warfare is commonly reinforced as territorial demonic spirits must be identified and then overcome to achieve victory in that area.

---

[39] Often referred to as Kingdom Now or Dominion Theology.
[40] Some key terms used are Manifest Sons of God and Joel's Army.

There are a lot of new things being incorporated in some churches. We have grave soaking, the idea that you can pick up someone's anointing, even if they are dead, by laying on their grave. We have gold, glitter, and feathers falling from the ceiling during worship service. We have signs, wonders, and miracles, some may be real, but many are staged. One man tells a story that he went to the grocery store and because the anointing on him was so strong; everyone in the entire grocery store fell over, apparently from the power of God that was on him in an instantaneous slain in the spirit movement.[41] Others are going to graveyards trying to raise the dead as Jesus did.

But one of the greatest dangers in this is that self-appointed prophets and apostles are coming to town. They hobnob and are endorsed by other self-appointed apostles, and each one runs their own territory. They are in charge of a group of churches in a particular area, and each pastor in that territory needs to submit to their apostolic authority. If they do not listen to or follow this apostolic authority, then they are out of the will of God, and he cannot facilitate the kingdom victories that need to happen, and of course, bad things will now happen. One does not have to look long and hard at the cults to see how this can become problematic. Who supervises these apostles? And why do we need to submit to these apostles when we are supposed to be submitting to Christ and being guided by His word? And what happens when we start putting feelings over the Bible, mysticism over theology, and apostles and prophets over scripture?

We have instructions from the Bible in regard to this:

> And if you say in your heart, "How may we
> know the word that the Lord has not spoken?"—
> when a prophet speaks in the name of the Lord,
> if the word does not come to pass or come true,

---

[41] Being "slain in the spirit" generally refers to a preacher or someone with a special anointing placing their hand on someone and the person falls backward or collapses due to being overcome by the power of the Holy Spirit.

that is a word that the Lord has not spoken; the prophet has spoken it presumptuously. You need not be afraid of him.[42]

And also:

> Beloved, do not believe every spirit, but test the spirits to see whether they are from God, for many false prophets have gone out into the world.[43]

Many of these "prophets" toss softball prophecies out. Someone in the room is struggling in life, and things will get better. Since this will likely impact over a third of the room, many people think it is geared for them. But some prophets get more specific. One prophet recently declared that God was going to flood the world a second time due to the sin in the world. Numerous prophets declared that Donald Trump would win the 2020 election. Self-appointed prophets across America make personal and public prophecies about individuals, jobs, and current events that do not come true. Some prophets are leading churches. Many of these prophets claim to be taking trips to heaven, talking to Jesus, and angels, and then delivering special prophetic messages. You cannot refute these messages as they are apparently coming right from Jesus Himself. The concern is that people can say literally anything, and you cannot really go against them because this prophet is hobnobbing with Jesus directly, and this means you would be speaking against God's anointed prophet.

Some churches are combining prophecies with financial declarations to really exert authority over the congregation. Declarations of future promotions or financial success are tied to giving a certain

---

[42] Deuteronomy 18:21–22 (ESV)
[43] 1 John 4:1 (ESV)

amount of money at a certain time. Paul writes to the church in Thessalonica:

Do not treat prophecies with contempt.
Test everything. Hold on to the good.[44]

So the Bible shows that Paul is not against the idea of prophecy but wants them tested. And the proper way to test prophecies would be to line them up with the Bible. If God were to speak through a person today, it would be in complete agreement with what God has already said in the Bible, as God does not contradict Himself.

Dear friends, do not believe every spirit, but
test the spirits to see whether they are from God,
because many false prophets have gone out into
the world.[45]

Now instead of weighing prophecies and testing them against the Word of God, and worrying if they line up to the Bible, we can simply just change the Bible. In many camps, special divine revelation from God supersedes the Bible itself. And we have a new Bible version that has started to do that. On one hand, it has beautiful imagery that seems to enhance the scriptures. But there are some problematic issues. It was produced by one author, who claimed to have received downloads of direct revelation from God as God breathed on him.[46] One of the most alarming aspects of this is that he claims to have gone to a library in heaven in a dream and attempted to shoplift the twenty-second chapter of the book of John as apparently we have not received this yet. He did not get it at this time, but God told him he would receive it at a later date, to add to the book of John.

---

[44] 1 Thessalonians 5:20–21
[45] 1 John 4:1 (ESV)
[46] Some of these inspired writings were later changed due to criticism from critics, which is a concern unto itself, as this: how is supposed divine revelation changed?

This chapter is supposed to bring in a new spiritual awakening and transformation of the church. While the current edition of *The Passion Translation* Bible does not have the twenty-second chapter of John, it does have numerous new verses that were added from divine direct revelation. It is a reworded and rewritten Bible, created to withhold a particular theology. Old Testament scholar Dr. Andrew Shead noted that so much new material was added "that it is at least 50 percent longer than the original."[47] What is concerning is that this is the same formula used by other cults such as the Mormons, Jehovah's Witnesses, etc. *from The Passion Translation*[48]:

> The meaning of a passage took priority
> over the form of the original words. Sometimes
> to communicate the correct intended meaning,
> words needed to be changed.[49]

The concern is that even if the language sounds beautiful or that it feels better when we are relying more on emotions, supposed divine revelation, and feelings over the original languages of the Bible that we already have, it is going to become problematic if it is not so already.

---

[47] The entire quote states that *The Passion Translation* is "Abandoning all interest in textual accuracy, playing fast and loose with the original languages, and inserting so much new material into the text that it is at least 50 percent longer than the original. The result is a strongly sectarian translation that no longer counts as Scripture; by masquerading as a Bible, it threatens to bind entire churches in thrall to a false god." Retrieved from A. Childers (n.d.), *Here's Why Christians Should Be Concerned about The Passion Translation of the Bible.* Alisa Childers. Retrieved April 4, 2023, from https://www.alisachildersblog.com/blog/heres-why-christians-should-be-concerned-about-the-passion-translation-of-the-bible.

[48] Today we have over twenty reliable translations to choose from including some older translations. The Message Translation is also problematic.

[49] GotQuestions.org. (2016, September 7). *Home.* GotQuestions.org. Retrieved February 22, 2023, from https://www.gotquestions.org/Passion-Translation.html.

Some people mistakenly believe the problem is just being Pentecostal/Charismatic. But that is not the problem. The problem is that in some churches, we have extra-biblical revelations that are being allowed to supersede the Word of God. Visions, dreams, and meetings with angels are taking precedence over established truth, logic, and the Bible. The Assemblies of God, the largest known Pentecostal/Charismatic branch in the United States, has formally rejected all forms of extra-biblical revelation[50] as do many other Pentecostal/Charismatic churches as they anchor their church on the Bible, the cross, and the gospel.

Pastor Keith Atwood is one of those churches that anchors his church on the Bible. He runs his church out of Lapeer, Michigan, and another new church plant in Pakistan. Pastor Keith is part of the Charismatic/Pentecostal movement. He enthusiastically embraces the movement yet recognizes that problems are coming out of this movement and outside this movement as well. People build them-selves up, idolatry, using earphones to deliver fake prophetic mes-sages, witchcraft, etc. He reminds us to look at Ephesians 4; everyone has a different role in the church.

Beware of traditions of men (religion) as traditions of men could have a controlling, highly political church where you have to submit to their way or you are out. Good leaders will surround themselves with a good nucleus. Beware of rebellion, lawlessness, and hobby horses. Sometimes a group will just start riding hobby horses. This leads to unbalance. Whether they are focused on end-times, proph-ecy, or prosperity, you cannot just focus on one thing and disregard other aspects as it leads to unbalance. Everything needs to be bal-anced in the body of Christ.

Pastor Keith believes in allowing more freedom and oppor-tunity for people in the church. He lets people get up and speak freely during certain times. Pastor Keith says that if God can speak through a donkey, God can speak through anyone. Pastor Keith

---

[50] While the headquarters at the Assemblies of God has rejected all extra-biblical revelation, each branch of the church does have some freedom to run the church under their own leadership.

warns us about getting legalistic, to beware of easy believism, and to beware of entertainment or seeker-friendly places. Some people are just building a kingdom and keeping money in their house for their own personal kingdom.

Pastor Keith says that while he enjoys looking at other pastors and listening to them, he is not a part of anyone else's camp; he says he is just in God's camp guided by the Bible. Pastor Keith enjoys working with other churches, sharing the pulpit, and helping other churches. He says that you just need to stay away from envy, jealousy, or pride. Pastor Keith runs a midweek prayer meeting on Tuesdays where five different churches are represented. He sees answered prayers, strengthened faith, and stronger community dynamics. They might read the word and worship a little, but it is prayer-focused and not church-focused, open to the community. He stays away from agendas and soapboxes.

Pastor Keith says we are in the Laodicean Church age. It is lukewarm, sleepy, full of compromise, and lethargic and lazy. Some of this is fear-driven. We are entering the great apostasy, the great falling away. He reminds us of 1 Timothy 4:1 (ESV):

> Now the Spirit expressly says that in later
> times some will depart from the faith by devot-
> ing themselves to deceitful spirits and teachings
> of demons.

Pastor Keith warns us to be aware of lawlessness, which the OSAS or "once saved, always saved" group can manipulate to support a lifestyle of unrepentant sin.[51] He reminds us about how Paul warned Corinth about problems which would lead to judgment. His final thoughts are to beware of institutions that allow people

---

[51] The theological implications of salvation and the arguments about whether you can remain a Christian and still be involved in unrepentant sin are not discussed in this book, as this is a frequently debated topic with entire books written on it from both perspectives. Both sides should be able to agree that using the "once saved, always saved" theory for justification and promotion of lawlessness is wrong and certainly contradicts scripture.

to become stuck, churches that appease conscience without results, or submitting to man's will. Also watch out for when the *anointed* becomes the *annoying*.

Pastor Mark Fibranz works on semitrucks during the week and runs his church, the Point Church, on Sundays. In response to emotionalism, or allowing emotions to control the direction of the church, Pastor Mark stated: "I am more skeptical of my feelings than anything else!" You have to decide between what is nice and what is the truth and a lot of the world is creeping into the church and gets labeled as *feelings*. He says that if someone does have a prophecy, the Word of God is the litmus test for this prophecy and that if someone claims to have a word from the Lord, it cannot contradict the Bible. While Pastor Mark stays busy with preaching and a full-time job, he still makes room for occasional counseling. One common area where he sees feelings overtaking reason is in marriages. Oftentimes, one party member will have legitimate feelings of anger and frustration and want to quit. They will then use these feelings and say that God told them to get a divorce. But Pastor Mark reminds them what the Bible says about divorce and looks to restore the marriage rather than end the marriage.

Pastor Mark brings up the story that we have in 1 Kings 13. In this chapter, we have a prophet who was referred to as a Man of God. He correctly delivers a prophecy to the King and then is told to not eat and drink before he gets home. The king offers him food and drink, but the prophet does the right thing and refuses this and heads home as God tells him to. On the way home, this young prophet encounters another prophet, an old prophet. This old prophet lies to the young prophet and tells him that he saw an angel which told him that it was okay for the young prophet to have food and water. The young prophet goes back to the old prophet's house and eats and drinks.

And then the word of the Lord comes again and lets the young prophet know that He will lose His life over this. So a lion comes and kills him later on. So we have one prophet, an old prophet who claims to be a prophet, claims to be delivering a word from the Lord and to have received a message from an angel, but this is a false prophecy and lie that actually kills the young prophet, the man of God. Going to the New Testament, Matthew warns us:

> Beware of false prophets, which come to you in sheep's clothing, but inwardly they are ravening wolves.[52]

Today we have self-appointed prophets in the church, some who are not prophets of God, delivering messages from angels or telling stories of visiting heaven and receiving special messages to deliver. Some of these are contrary to the Bible and the gospel message. Scripture makes it clear that we are not to follow emotions, the latest new thing, or anybody who claims to be receiving special divine revelation from God, but rather His special revelation that we already have, which is the Bible. Some churches are allowing emotions to break themselves free from the biblical anchor they were previously tied to.

Music has been used to stir up emotions across cultures ever since humans arrived on the scene. Pastor Terry Smith likes to talk about the emotional impact of music in the church today. He preaches out of New Beginnings Missionary Baptist Church in Tampa. Tampa is a fun city with lots of activities right on the bay with a really neat riverwalk. It seems to draw people who like the urban culture and the recreational opportunities the city affords. For whatever reason, winning sports teams are also drawn to the area.

Pastor Terry worries about excess emotionalism in our worship music that is heading away from actual worship. He says worship music is designed to elicit emotions. Look at David, and look at Psalms; we need to worship. He is worried that some of the songs played in churches with powerful bands, light shows, and semiprofessional musicians do elicit strong emotions in people, but some of it is not worship.

A recent study took thirty popular Christian songs and had random people read the lyrics. Many thought the songs were just roman-

---

[52] Matthew 7:15 (KJV)

tic love songs and did not even recognize that they were Christian worship songs. Pastor Terry says there is absolutely nothing wrong with modern songs, but pastors have to make sure that they hit the mark. So Pastor Terry sometimes goes back to the classics; he goes back to the hymns. "Amazing Grace" is his favorite.

"Amazing Grace" was composed by John Newton who was a sailor involved in the slave trade. Sailors could be a rough lot, but Newton had a reputation for profanity, coarseness, and debauchery which shocked even his fellow sailors. Newton gave his life to God and had a transformed life. The song laments what a miserable wretch he was and how we are lost, blind in sin, and need saving. He later quit the slave trade and passionately and frequently spoke against it, which helped lead to the abolition of the slave trade in Britain. In his later years, as his memory was fading, he stated: "My memory is nearly gone; but I remember two things: That I am a great sinner, and that Christ is a great Savior."[53]

Pastor Jeremy Neff reminds us that emotions themselves are not a bad thing; the problem is when we allow these emotions to supersede the Word of God. Pastor Jeremy preaches out of Heritage Christian Fellowship in Oregon. Some of the Midwesterners see Oregon as developing into another liberal utopia along the coast to rival California. But a lot of that is limited to the main cities. Oregon has some of the most scenic coastline in America along with Crater Lake which is a lake that formed at the top of a blown-off volcano, also Columbia River which includes a gorge, both of which include some must-see scenery. While the winters tend to be cloudy and wet, the summers are nice with almost a Mediterranean-type feel to them.

Pastor Jeremy understands the backlash regarding emotions that we are seeing in some places throughout the church. And he offers another perspective. Some Christians are taught that emotions are bad; as a result of that, there can be an unhealthy atmosphere. People are not equipped to grieve and do not know how to deal with

---

[53] D. Severance, *When John Newton Discovered Amazing Grace (and Wrote the Hymn)*, (Christianity.com, 2022, September 2), Retrieved February 28, 2023, from https://www.christianity.com/church/church-history/timeline/1701-1800/john-newton-discovered-amazing-grace-11630253.html.

the anger. It creates a toxic positivity. Some churches have overcorrected this and have created environments where feeling good is what you are in pursuit of; it is the primary focus—laser lights, dynamic music, playing on physiological and emotional states.

But there is a middle road to all this. God does feel our anger, sorrow, emotions, grief, and loss—the full range of human emotions. Those who are met to bear His image are going to have those feelings too. We can take our feelings and offer them to Him. Look at the range of emotions that we see in David in the book of Psalms. We have the book of Lamentations and the anguish of the prophets. God wants an honest cry of the heart.

Pastor Jeremy reminds us to look at the imprecatory psalms. The imprecatory psalms are filled with emotion; they imprecate or invoke judgment and anger on those who are perceived as enemies of God. In some places, the author hates his enemies. Psalm 69 seems to show almost the full range of human emotion with:

> Save me, O God; for the waters are come in
> unto my soul. I sink in deep mire, where there is
> no standing: I am come into deep waters, where
> the floods overflow me. I am weary of my crying:
> my throat is dried: mine eyes fail while I wait for
> my God.[54]

David is distraught and grieving. Then he goes into:

> Pour out thine indignation upon them, and
> let thy wrathful anger take hold of them. Let
> their habitation be desolate; and let none dwell
> in their tents. For they persecute him whom thou
> hast smitten; and they talk to the grief of those
> whom thou hast wounded. Add iniquity unto

---

[54] Psalm 69:1–3 (KJV)

their iniquity: and let them not come into thy
righteousness.[55]

The psalm concludes with praise:

> Let the heaven and earth praise him, the
> seas, and every thing that moveth therein.[56]

David encountered a wide range of emotions. Jesus shows us he had emotions also, especially before His crucifixion. Having emotions is how God created us, they are not wrong unto themselves. We see in Psalms that God records this anguish. And we can take the truest part of what we feel and offer it up to God. It offers a release, rather than somebody who is carrying out justice on their own. This shows us an example of what to do with your feelings: offer them back to God. God knows our heart, we cannot hide it, and we can only offer what is true.

There is no craving for emotional experiences when we are emotionally healthy; we do not have to manufacture them. But we have to remember that God's word will remain forever and is the highest cord of authority. Anybody who thinks they have a new revelation that supersedes scripture is mistaken or deceived. Pastor Jeremy reminds us what Paul said to the church in Corinth:

> Let the prophets speak two or three, and let
> the other judge.[57]

We are to judge based on what has already been revealed by the Word of God. Our emotions are healed, restored, and healthy when they are aligned with God and the Word of God.

---

[55] Psalm 69:24–27 (KJV)
[56] Psalm 69:34 (KJV)
[57] 1 Corinthians 14:29 (KJV)

7

Conformity in Christ

The First World War was a tremendously gruesome affair as America along with many other countries found itself in its first global war. At times, the loss of life and medical injuries were so severe that hospital staff simply could not keep up with them. So in 1918, the United States adopted the French method of *triage*. This turned out to be an effective method to sort, classify, move around, and determine essential care so that initial treatment could begin for the soldiers. A soldier with a missing limb would be moved up for emergency urgent care while another soldier with a broken pinky or some sort of shell shock or psychological trauma would be moved to another area for care that would be addressed later. It was all-important, and all the care mattered to the medical staff; they had to just determine what type of care was essential and to be taken care of immediately and what was not.

Pastor Aaron Newman runs a church out of California, and he talks about a theological triage. This helps to identify what is essential and what is not in the church.

First-tier issues are going to be essential doctrines of the Christian faith—the gospel, the trinity, the concept that God was fully God and fully man, the authority of the scriptures, and the life, death, burial, and resurrection of Jesus Christ, His atonement for our sins, etc. This does not mean that we find fault if someone is not educated on a topic, but if you deny these first-tier issues, you essentially deny Christ.

Second-tier issues are going to divide us into different churches but should never divide us as Christians. This could be baptism, infant baptism, circumcision, if a baby enters into a new covenant, etc. This is a healthy division. Churches can create different churches or denominations over some of these issues, but it is crucial to remember that we are still one in the body of Christ.

Third-tier issues are going to lead to some theological differences, but you are generally still going to be in the same church. And you should be able to get along. This would be something like eschatological[58] views or various nonessential interpretations in the Bible.

A division in some cases can be healthy, as long as you recognize that you are still one in the body of Christ. A church in another city with a different worship style is not a competitor but rather should be looked at as someone who aims to accomplish the same goal. There can be healthy divisions. One problem that Pastor Aaron mentions is that there is a danger of people who want to divide over issues that are not first- and second-tier issues. Another concern is people who do not clearly deny critical issues but present teachings contrary to them. Pastor Aaron reminds us that you do not have to swim in vocabulary, but you should understand and have familiarity with essential doctrinal issues and statements of faith. One thing that we need to do is minimize the overemphasis on doctrinal differences which has led to division in the body of Christ.

Pastor Aaron Newman believes that a good church is going to have church discipline as you need biblical church discipline to honor the name of Christ. While something like greed might be hard to address, if you are in an ongoing rebellion against God or in some type of public sin, it needs to be addressed. And do not partake in communion if you are in sin. This can bring dishonor to the glory of God. The objective here is to bring them to repentance and get them under some type of discipleship. They will also practice ordinances, which refer to the laws and commandments of God. Also exposi-

---

[58] Another term for interpretations of the end-times.

tory preaching which ensures that the preaching overviews the entire Bible. If the preaching is not from the Bible, it is a problem. If there is a lack of theology, there is often a lack of expository preaching.

Pastor Aaron Newman sees the full gospel message as a concise way to share the truth. He starts off with God and a reminder that he exists and is all-powerful. He then covers the fall of man, Adam in the Garden, and the introduction of sin into the world. Then he covers the good news of Jesus, who was sent as the snake crusher, and his penal substitutionary atonement, covering our sins. He says people should have a biblical understanding of conversion, and it really should be incorporated into every sermon. He states that involvement in a church can lead to greater clarity and contribute to your overall spiritual health. While running a church always creates plenty of opportunities for division, Pastor Aaron has found that expository preaching throughout the entire Bible does limit people from handpicking various verses to wing at each other and split over.

Pastor Bruce Shields is a pastor, author, and the vice president of the Iosco County Ministerial Association. This association seeks to unite all the churches in the area so that they are unified as one force and to go out and evangelize the community together. He states that oftentimes when one church goes and does this, members of the community think that the church is just trying to recruit more people to join the church, which is oftentimes the case; they see through it. But when multiple churches do it together to help the community and focus on the community and then tell them they are not recruiting them to their church, but there is a network of churches that they can go to, it creates less resistance from the community.

As the vice president of the Iosco County Ministerial Association, Pastor Shields has really enjoyed being able to network with other ministers and work together to encourage and uplift each other as they encounter similar problems. He stated that the association has a minimal requirement for entry, which is the Apostles' Creed. He states that the Apostles' Creed was formed to establish the minimal standards of the faith and has been used for centuries to weed out churches that do not meet these requirements. Churches need to agree with the creed to join. All the churches that belong to this association have. One church in particular acknowledges the creed but refuses to join the association because they believe that they are the only way to salvation. As discussed previously, when your church or group sees itself as the only answer and the only way to salvation, you might be in a theological cult. One issue that originally caused conflict in this association was regarding speaking in tongues, as some members wanted to participate in it at the meetings, and some did not. Pastor Bruce said that he resolved this issue by allowing tongues but only with an interpreter as stated in Corinthians.[59]

Pastor Shields has noted that in many churches, there is a falling away. You still need to be faithful and present the word. Stay as close to the word and truth as possible. Get away from man's doctrines of denominations and stick to the Bible as the Word of God. Follow what the early church does in Acts. He states that if it is "Good enough for the First Century, it is good enough for today." The danger today is that we cannot focus so much on entertainment that we forget about the truth of His word.

Pastor Bruce stated that the body of Christ needs to grow and that we need to do what we are called to do. Pastor Shields personally tries evangelization and relational discipleship but is hoping that a revivalist or evangelist comes to the area soon to stir up some of the people. He stated that there are only two types of people in the world, those who have the Lord and those who do not. Our job is to bring more people into the latter camp, and we need to crucify the flesh and get rid of selfish ambitions to do this.

Pastor Bruce Shields' final thought for the churches is to bring a balance to the church. Some churches rely all on the Bible, which is good, but they reject the things of the Spirit. Other churches focus solely on the Spirit and experiences, but they reject the words of the Bible. We need to be open to the Holy Spirit and the things of God while having our foundation firmly rooted in the Word of God. Pastor Bruce looks forward to uniting churches and setting people

---

[59] "If any speak in a tongue, let there be only two or at most three, and each in turn, and let someone interpret. But if there is no one to interpret, let each of them keep silent in church and speak to himself and to God." (1 Corinthians 14:27–28 ESV)

free. He escaped bondage himself as he grew up in a gang and drug culture that was around him as a kid. He found the Lord, and God pulled him out of that environment. He was able to rescue his mom and pull her out of that lifestyle too.

There have been a lot of second- and third-tier issues that have caused division in the body of Christ. And for the most part, many of these issues should have provided intellectually stirring debates, rather than division. Certain eschatological beliefs concerning the rapture, tribulation, and the timing of Christ's return have always been trigger issues. When does a rapture take place on the timeline? And some groups do not even believe in a rapture. Fancy words such as *pre-trib*, *post-trib*, and *amillennialism* are talked about, and camps are created. Jacob Arminius was supposed to give a sermon defending John Calvin's idea of Calvinism. During his research, he found he could not defend Calvins's ideas of predestination and unconditional election, so now we have Arminianism.

Whether you are reformed[60] or not is starting to cause some tension in some areas and even division in others. There are also divisions between churches on styles of worship. Some churches divide along political, racial, or economic lines. Denominations are created so now we can also divide the body of Christ among denominational lines, whether that is Baptist, Lutheran, Apostolic, Presbyterian, Pentecostal, Calvinist, Methodist, etc. Sometimes, it just seems that many churches are in competition on who has the best buildings and programs.

We need more unity in the body of Christ, not division. Churches need to be united more and come together more, rather than look at each other as enemies or competition. Of course, this is not a rallying cry for universalism where all of the world's religions are one as we hold hands, talk about love, and sing "Kumbaya" in a globalistic march toward universal acceptance. We need to acknowl-

---

[60] Being reformed is generally going to mean that you affirm the five solas, the gospel, are creedal, covenantal, and confessional. Some reformed believers are also Calvinists. TULIP is a Calvinistic principle that has five points. Some Calvinists believe in all five points, while others may only agree with four of the points, so they would be considered a four-point Calvinist.

edge that other people might have different opinions, and while we should research the Bible to gain a better understanding of what the truth is, we need to understand that there may be a difference of opinion on nonessential items.

They can still be enthusiastically debated but just as a brother in Christ, and not an enemy. They may still be important, but they are nonessential. Likewise, if a church does not agree with essential items like the atonement, that Christ Jesus came to the earth as a propitiation for our sins and our salvation, we need to recognize that they are outside the body of Christ. Removing or twisting the atonement means that you do not meet the biblical definition of Christianity according to the Bible. Simply calling yourself a church does not meet the minimal qualifications of being a church, as wearing a golf shirt does not necessarily mean you are a golfer.

One common division that we see in the church today seems to occur between the Pentecostal/Charismatic camp and those that are not in this camp. Your Pentecostal/Charismatic camp is going to see some dreams, supernatural healings, speaking in tongues, prophecies, words from the Lord, and deliverance, as miracles for today, along with other supernatural encounters. Other people are more cessationists, which is a doctrine that spiritual gifts such as tongues, prophecy, and healing ceased with the apostolic age.[61]

Pentecostal/Charismatic churches that are anchored in God's word seem to bring a lot of excitement, enthusiasm, and energy along with passionate prayer. They enjoy sharing stories about miraculous healings and about how God has delivered people out of various bondages. They can be great churches as long as they remain anchored in biblical truth. Your non-Pentecostal/Charismatic camp often delivers robust intellectually inspired sermons that help keep their congregants anchored in the faith. Many churches are doctrinally sound and biblically anchored resulting in strong family units.

But what is interesting is that there are no hard and fast rules on this. Some churches pick different bits and aspects that they follow or

---

[61] Most cessationists believe the miraculous gift signs ceased with the apostolic age but that God can still occasionally work in the supernatural today.

don't. And congregants are left to pick their own views, which may differ slightly from the church they belong to, as many people have moved between camps to find what aligns with their beliefs.

But we need to remember that these are not first-tier views worth dividing over. It is not so much the differences between them but rather the truth that ties them together through the cross. You could belong to a noncharismatic church and enjoy it very much. But it would not hurt you to go visit a charismatic church. Maybe take a trip to Cajun country and visit Pastor Tony Spells'[62] church. He delivers biblically inspired, poetical sermons with plenty of energy as he bolts across the congregation. It will have a different feel to it. Try to sit an entire sermon without moving. First, your knee will start tapping just a little, your head will start bobbing, and maybe you start clapping a little. By the end of it you might be yelling "Amen" and getting all excited. But your faith will be encouraged; you will be inspired.

Likewise, if you go to a Pentecostal/Charismatic group, listen to someone from the other camp a few times, turn on an intellectually vigorous and stimulating sermon from someone like Paul Washer, John Piper, or Alistair Begg, or read something from one of the greatest from the past like Spurgeon, Luther, or Whitefield, or someone from this book. Get anchored in the truth. You will find that these biblically based robust sermons can be just as exciting and strengthen your faith. Both camps can learn from each other, rather than be afraid of each other, as long as they are both solid Bible-believing gospel-preaching churches.

What is interesting is during the COVID crisis, two pastors in the United States drew the most nationwide media attention for not closing down due to COVID and continued to fight after facing pressure to close down. They were Tony Spell and John MacArthur, both from different camps, but in reality, it is the same camp.[63]

---

[62] Pastor Tony Spell will be properly introduced later in this book.

[63] John Macarthur won eight hundred thousand over his legal battle with the state of California over the forced church shut downs as he kept his church open while California tried to force it to close withstanding constant media and state pressure. He stated, "The biblical order is clear: Christ is Lord over

If anyone could feel the momentum to cater to a particular group, it would likely be Dr. Kirt Anderson who pastors a church in sunny Naples, Florida. His church can be found in Collier County. Collier County is 60 to 70 percent Republican and 10 percent Libertarian which generally ends up voting Republican. He has a current Republican State Senator and former Republican Governor that go to his church. You would think that when you walk into his church, you would see giant inflatable elephants and have to sign an agreement to always love the Republican party as they play the official soundtrack of the Republican National Convention during worship time.

But Dr. Kirt Anderson hates all divisions which would include church division but also political division. Dr. Kirt Anderson says that you need to focus on preaching from the pulpit and ignore cultural or political references. Politics can put a lot of pressure on you and lead to an abuse of the pulpit. Do not use the pulpit as a soapbox for your political beliefs. We are supposed to be upstream from both culture and politics. Do not cater your message to a political narrative. The political world is guilty of hijacking profound moral issues and making them into pure politics. Stay away from it and completely focus on preaching the gospel.

Pastor Kirt says he appreciates the whole church growth movement and appreciates those who have done it, but they are doing the process wrong. He recalls his seminary professor from Princeton hammering home the message to preach the word. Preach the word. You are under the word. If you preach the rightly preached word through the power of Christ, it will all come together. We need to focus on building our Christian identity and living with that during the week, not just on Sunday morning. Pastor Kirt worries about some churches that are becoming apostate churches. There is a denominational drift as they head more toward social issues and

---

Caesar, not vice versa. Christ, not Caesar, is head of the church." Pastor Tony Spell also won his challenges in Louisiana, though the federal government still has security cameras put up for traffic that are also facing his private residence that he wants removed.

away from the pressures of culture and politics. The church is losing power due to conforming to the culture.

Pastor Kirk reminds us about times when the church fought back against the culture and pressure around it. Down in Cuba, they have the Las Damas de Blanco, where ladies dressed in all white come out to silently protest their husbands being imprisoned by the government. They acted in a way that was appropriate in the Christian faith while standing against the pressures of the government. Many in the German church caved to Nazi-ism. They had taken Germanic cultural vows to be faithful to the government and got caught in between; they learned compliance by silence, while a remnant remained faithful to the truth. And we have the reformation where government power and church abuse collided with truth. When the church gets too much power, it is a corrupting influence. The church is to be reflective of the person of Christ and should not be hungry to be in tight association with power but rather stick to the real work of the gospel.

Pastor Kirt worries that some mainline churches have become all about property, power, and money. But he believes that we should love anyone, with no doctrinal barrier, and avoid dividing over the things of the world. He reminds us that we have all sinned and fallen short of the glory of God and make no pretense of righteousness and understand that the law is to spread the love of Christ in the neighborhood, not the law of division. Meet with love and not doctrine.

8

Does Truth Matter?

Sometimes truth is not always the objective. Sometimes people take the truth and then batter, beat, and mold it into their own version of what they want the truth to be. There is a term for this; it is called false teaching. False teaching is not something new it has been around since the time of Christ, really before Christ. The Old Testament is littered with countless stories and examples of kings, prophets, or people leading people away from the teachings of God. Individuals and Israel as a nation would continually get off track, realize they made a mistake, and burn their false gods, then later go back to these same gods down the road. Countless teachers would continually pull individuals and the nation of Israel in the wrong direction.

These things just did not disappear during the time of Christ but rather appeared to grow in strength. Jesus frequently spoke against deceivers, frauds, and false teachers. Paul addressed this in countless letters to the churches. In fact, there are 196 verses[64] warning us about false teaching.[65] Warnings about false teachers are listed in every book of the New Testament excluding the book of Philemon.

---

[64] *196 Bible Verses about False Teachers*. Bible Portal. (n.d.). Retrieved October 25, 2023, from https://bibleportal.com/topic/false-teachers.

[65] *What Does the Bible Say About Exposing False Teachers?* (n.d.). Www.openbible. info. Retrieved February 3, 2023, from https://www.openbible.info/topics/ exposing_false_teachers#:~:text=100%20Bible%20Verses%20about%20 Exposing%20False%20Teachers%201.

So it is not as much if we will encounter them, but when we will encounter them.

> But false prophets also arose among the people, just as there will be false teachers among you, who will secretly bring in destructive heresies, even denying the Master who bought them, bringing upon themselves swift destruction.[66]

> For such men are false apostles, deceitful workmen, disguising themselves as apostles of Christ. And no wonder, for even Satan disguises himself as an angel of light. So it is no surprise if his servants, also, disguise themselves as servants of righteousness. Their end will correspond to their deeds.[67]

> Beware of false prophets, who come to you in sheep's clothing but inwardly are ravenous wolves. You will recognize them by their fruits. Are grapes gathered from thornbushes, or figs from thistles? So, every healthy tree bears good fruit, but the diseased tree bears bad fruit. A healthy tree cannot bear bad fruit, nor can a diseased tree bear good fruit. Every tree that does not bear good fruit is cut down and thrown into the fire.[68]

Pastor Ben Whittinghill is up in New England and preaches out of Rivertown Church in Vermont. Vermont is a cold but beautiful state up in the corner of America by Maine. It really looks like one state that was jaggedly cut in half with New Hampshire, a beau-

------

[66] 2 Peter 2:1 (ESV)

[67] 2 Corinthians 11:13–15 (ESV)

[68] Matthew 7:15–20 (ESV)

tifully landscaped state with heavily wooded areas and trails with lots of snow in the winter, more snow than anywhere else in America. Pastor Ben says that false teachers teach this way because they are this way themselves. They enjoy stroking the feelings and desires of people to get them hooked. And they pervert the grace of God into sensuality, that God is so gracious that you can stay in your sin without changing anything or repenting.

Pastor Ben likes to remind us about Romans 6 and 1 John 1–2, the perseverance of the saints, and that God is not going to lose one of them. If you trust in Jesus, real faith will change you. There should be a desire to obey, everyone is going to do that imperfectly, and it is going to look different, but we should have that desire. Strive to be perfect and Christlike, but when you do sin, you have an advocate, and this advocate is the propitiation for the world. Pastor Ben likes to remind us about Romans 5–6: Do not deceive yourself. God's grace is so lavish that we cannot outsin it. But does that mean that someone who is truly saved should continue to sin or strive to sin as much as they can? No, God forbid. How can we who have died still live in sin? We need to pursue the holiness and fear of God.

Pastor Ben is worried about theological liberalism invading the church. Theological liberalism is a branch of Christianity that interprets scripture in light of liberalism and interprets it given the culture. Reason and experience trump the Bible. He uses the US Constitution as an example. Look at how many people today are trying to interpret it to fit their own desires, goals, and views. Pastor Ben says that people are trying to do that with the Bible. What does it mean to you, and how do you interpret that text? But it is not up to us on how we interpret the text or on how it makes us feel, but rather, what God said when he originally wrote it. The word cannot be changed.

Theological liberalism is the height of what man can do and has accomplished. But God does not change, the gospel does not change, and we need to contend for the faith.

Theological liberalism is incredibly dangerous as it seeks to change the nature of sin. Theological liberalism works to take a detour around the cross. Instead of the cross changing you, you are going to change the nature of God.

Pastor Ben reminds us that the Bible tells us not to judge, and this is good. But he also reminds us that if we are just telling people what God has already said, you are not a judge; He is. You are just a messenger delivering the truth of God, not your opinion.

> The times of ignorance God overlooked, but now he commands all people everywhere to repent, because he has fixed a day on which he will judge the world in righteousness by a man whom he has appointed; and of this he has given assurance to all by raising him from the dead.[69]

This message to repent is not really a popular message. Jesus, John the Baptist, and Paul were all killed because of it.

But there is a fixed day, and at one point, everyone is going to be judged, not by a person, not by you, not by the church, but by almighty God. This is an amazing truth, a terrifying fear. He is alive, and you will stand naked and give an account; bow now or later. Pastor Ben reminds us that he is not judging anyone. You should not judge anyone, but there is a judge. Correctly deliver God's message in truth and love.

Pastor Ben reminds us that the church is our source of truth. And the church must hold the line for truth. The church is responsible to speak truth, confront, call out, and explain the judgment that everyone will encounter one day. God is the judge; He judges. Pastor Ben reminds us to read Hebrews chapter 10. Gather to encourage. Exhort. Do not harden. Do not water down the message or be lukewarm. Jesus came to save sinners. We are sanctified but not holy. We will have sin. Let us hold fast, stand up, and be obedient. It is okay to feel scared but push through. Find a church, preach the Bible, preach sin, preach the cross, and preach faithfully.

---

[69] Acts 17:30–31 (ESV)

Pastor Ben says to reread Colossians 1–3, Ephesians 1–3, and really most of Paul's letters. This shows us how to set our minds above and live out the faith. Be a disciple of the gospel and light of Christ. Live out the faith. Set your mind above. This is not for your own personal private religion. Put off the old and put on the new. Forgive, be patient, kind, humble, and love. He reminds us that it is going to be hard to defend truth in the modern world. But you need to examine the truth itself in the Bible so you know where there is error and how to defend it.

Many Christians will be led away by false teachers. Jesus Christ himself warned us about this. Be alert and stay entrenched in the truth. Pastor Ben once heard of someone who was afraid to study theology as he did not want to *dry up*. But real love does not survive not knowing. You do not love your wife less by not knowing her more. More study will lead to becoming more enthralled, not more stoic and dry. "In spirit *or* in truth" is a false dichotomy; do both.

Pastor Tyler Wilson pastors a church out in Oklahoma, the state that looks like a hatchet, known for its cowboy culture and Native American history. Pastor Tyler loves the Bible and has seen lives transformed through the Bible. But he is worried about the attacks that he sees taking place against it, attacks that are oftentimes unnoticed or not addressed. One of the many arms attacking the Bible and the church is progressive Christianity. Progressive Christianity comes off as sympathetic, but it declares warfare against traditional Christianity. Progressive Christianity seeks to blend the postmodern era with traditional Christianity. Led by Rob Bell and Jen Hatmaker, it started with the emergent church movement, which seeks to emerge beyond traditional Christianity and conform to the culture as the culture changes.

Pastor Tyler talks about how the emergent church movement really came about in response to popular church culture. We had the modern movement of megachurches, concerts, and the attractional movement. People were showing up as consumers, and it really had no relevance to modern-day issues. It left a large distaste in people's mouths. It was not all based on the Bible but more on cultural or social trends sprinkled with biblical phrases. The emergent church movement came out of this culture. It originally came out as very non-mainstream. Certain core tenets of Christianity were denied or hidden. It went underground for a bit, and as social practices became more prevalent in culture, with the rise of cultural relativity, what was hidden underground exploded and went mainstream. It reemerged in a popular fashion.

Progressive Christianity, evolved from the emergent church movement. It is hard to define. You cannot summarize it in a phrase or paragraph. It is hard to say what they are against. But essentially, every false gospel pretends to be gospel. Every false gospel either redefines sin or salvation. Progressive Christianity has a few tenets. At a high level, it embraces uncertainty, in place of absolute truth. The highest virtue is to doubt; doubt replaces faith. Progressive Christianity loves what God loves but does not hate what God hates.

The eroding of scriptures as absolute truth and as the final authority is important. The character of God is redefined. God's response to sin which is wrath and to seek justice is eliminated. God's love is redefined as wholesale acceptance. Love is redefined into a cultural version of tolerance; it becomes an endorsement. The character of God and the gospel gets redefined. Humans are not sinners in need of redemption; they just need more self-esteem, more self-confidence, and maybe some therapy. Others might take it as more of a social trend. There is oppression in the world, whether it is racial, economic, or based on social status, so we need to reverse the oppression in the world.

Moral issues generally associated with traditional Christianity are now redefined. The inerrancy of Scripture, the character of God, the gospel message, and ethics, and most moral issues are hidden, changed, or eliminated. Absolute truth is eliminated as you question everything and doubt becomes the new faith. With no absolute truth, the scriptures and the gospel are constantly redefined and deconstructed as the cultural climate changes. Core doctrinal truths get redefined as Jesus becomes more of a good moral teacher, rather than a redeemer from sin. There are various strains and different languages. It is very deceptive and rooted in Christian language. You end up with a Christianity that never offends and never challenges a God that is never glorified and a God that is just like you.

Pastor Tyler reminds us that the best thing to do is acknowledge it. Every member is confronted with it every day. Friends, coworkers, and church members are bombarded with it. Pastor Tyler is in the midst of a Bible belt, and it is still an issue, even with friends that he is close with; it is in his news feed every day. It is very cryptic, is very vague, and has its own language. You have to know what the lie is, and why it is counterfeit, then present the truth. You can ignore it, but then no one is getting equipped to combat it.

Pastor Tyler was asked why many pastors are not addressing this. He said that first off, it is a lot of work. You are asking them not only to study the Bible but also to look at all the current cultural trends and how they contradict the Bible, so you are some type of anthropologist or sociologist or something. The second reason is confidence. It is a hard study and takes a lot of precision. You do not want to mischaracterize the opposing side. You have to get your tone right. You do not want to be arrogant. You must be precise, and bold, but yet humble at the same time. The final reason is just fear, fear of man, and fear of the consequences of speaking the truth.

Pastor Tyler reminds us about the book of Titus which speaks to false gospels, and it speaks to American culture. But for a Christian, you cannot be pulled into silence. You must speak. But you also cannot be hateful, bigoted, prejudiced, intolerant, and unloving. You have to be confident and say things in the right manner; the spirit in which you say them is important. Do it on a relational level, that you are personally concerned for them, that you care for them, and that you are concerned that they are being deceived. The "us versus them" or "you are wrong, and I am right" mentality does not work regarding helping others.

Pastor Tyler explains that this is going to continue to be an issue. There is going to be a desire to preach relativism and tolerance. One of the local churches in Pastor Tyler's area did not want to lose people so they started compromising on various issues and becoming more progressive. The Pastor was confronted about it and did not want to change, so people left to go to other churches including

Pastor Tyler's church. You are starting to see this with some churches catering to those who want to remain in a biblically strong church while others are catering to those who want to have their ears tickled. The problem with the churches that are catering to the world is that while you will see a lot of people coming in the front door, you will see just as many people coming out the back door.

Pastor Tyler noted there are at least a dozen false gospels that we are seeing today in the church as modern counterfeits to Christ crucified outside the progressive gospel. We have the legalistic gospel which implies that you can find salvation through church attendance, Bible reading, tithing, missions, cultural customs, good deeds, etc., which creates more of a performance-driven Christianity. We have the moralistic gospel where God becomes more of a Santa Claus, and if you are a good boy you get to go to heaven, but if you are a bad boy you have to go to hell. So with God's help, we can move from good people to better people through the exercise of our willpower and maybe a little help from Jesus.

We have the fire-insurance gospel which says that as long as you say the sinners pray at some point, you are good. Being saved does not really impact your life, but that is okay because you have already completed everything you needed to accomplish in Christianity by saying that prayer. Save things like remorse for sin, evangelization, or the joy over the beauty of the gospel for the spiritual elite. Everything comes from saying the right phrases or following a formula, so it is almost a little more like witchcraft than Christianity.

We have the therapeutic/self-help and the prosperity gospels, which we covered previously. We have the experiential gospel which puts our experiences, feelings, and emotions over the objective truth of the gospel. We have the social justice gospel where our chief goal is to help those in poverty and those who are being treated unjustly. So an important byproduct of the gospel, social justice, becomes the ultimate priority over the true gospel message of sin and salvation. We have the universalistic gospel which attempts to align all the faiths together regardless of the differences. It ignores the exclusivity of the cross of Christ claim but fuses the love aspects of Christianity with other religions.

Pastor Tyler talks about the social club gospel where salvation is found in finding fellowship and friendship at church. Christianity is just a country club of relationships that helps us enjoy life more and develop deeper personal relationships. We have the knowledge gospel, where Christianity flows up to only those who have the greatest intellectual knowledge or fanciest degrees, resulting in an overtly academic and heartless approach to Christianity. And of course, we have the cults that spend more time controlling and twisting the truth, than allowing you to find it. All these false and distorted gospels seek to redefine the greatest problem. So they talk about a lack of money, education, self-belief, a better job, etc. instead of the greatest problem, which is sin. They will also redefine the solution, more self-esteem, resources, money, education, political power, and circumstances, instead of the real solution, which is more Jesus.

Anytime you try to address false teaching or point people toward Biblical truth, there is going to be pushback. The first one is "Do not touch God's anointed" and implies that anyone who speaks against these people is committing blasphemy. The statement comes from 1 Chronicles 16:22 and Psalms 105:15. They are frequently quoted in some circles as core doctrinal truths. The idea is that if someone speaks against these people, bad things will happen to them. It is more of a threat that God is going to attack their health or finances, rather than the idea that an elder is going to get the tire iron out of his trunk. This, of course, helps protect these preachers from scrutiny and allows them to spread bad theology and false teachings without the Bible getting in the way. It is also meant to instill fear in people who are speaking against false teaching, or "God's anointed."

And you should never speak against God's anointed. But some of the people quoting this are not God's anointed, so the quote does not apply to them. The second is that proclaiming truth is not frowned upon in scripture but rather commanded. And the final point is that those verses are referring to the patriarchs of God. David is giving a condensed review of the miraculous history of Israel and God's plan for Abraham, Isaac, and Jacob. No one was going to derail that plan, including the kings of Egypt and Canaan. David also refuses to touch God's anointed king Saul in 1 Samuel 26:9–11. Again, these verses deal with the protection God has on the patriarchs and those he rises up as rulers, nothing about questioning a speaker about false teaching. All believers today are God's anointed, set apart for the work God is accomplishing in this world. "Do not be an accuser of the brethren" is a spin-off of this.

Fear is the primary driving force in many areas—fear that if you do not give enough money, God will curse you, fear that if you do not say the right phrases, God will not act on your behalf, fear that if you express concerns about teaching, God will rain judgment down on you or not bless you. Some of these pastors will even go as far as to make declarations and "prophecies" that the enemy is going to rise up against anyone who speaks against the church.

Moving away from the fear category, the next point that gets brought up is that God is love. He is. But in some places, you are not really talking about love but rather using love as an endorsement and call for tolerance. That is not love. Just because God is love (He is) does not mean that He loves and endorses all sin. God is also righteous, holy, and our judge. A church can manipulate love. They love you if you comply and are submissive, but if not, you will encounter the wrath of the religious institution.

Sometimes, phrases such as "Do you think you are perfect?" or "Use discernment" can be used. So always be kind, loving, and humble, and speak the truth to people not because you are better than them but to rescue them. The idea that you need to obtain perfection to speak truth is silly. If that were the case, no one would do anything as Christ is the only person to have achieved perfection. Rather, it is a command given to us by scripture. Strawman arguments[70] and selective scriptures are commonly used. Sometimes an acknowledgment will be made that the teaching is wrong, but you need to just stay silent. Just keep everything hidden. So phrases such as "Do not say things in public," "Do not mention names," and "Do not tear down the body of Christ" are brought up.

Do not judge is one of the most brought-up points. And while we certainly cannot judge people in the world, they are living life as it makes most sense to them, and we cannot judge people's souls. Only

---

[70] A strawman argument is the logical fallacy of distorting an opposing position into an extreme version of itself and then arguing against that extreme version.

God can do that. We are commanded to judge the teachings inside the church. Paul writes to the church in Corinth that:

> What business is it of mine to judge those outside the church? Are you not to judge those inside? God will judge those outside. "Expel the wicked person from among you."[71]

Paul Washer's famous response to this phrase is: "Twist scripture not, lest you be like Satan."

Jesus teaches us how to judge in Matthew 7:1–6, commands us to judge in John 7:24, and shows us that it is the character of being spiritual in 1 Corinthians 2:15–16. Matthew 7:15–16 says that we are to judge false teachers, and 1 Corinthians 14:29 commands us to judge prophecy. We need to judge carefully,[72] correctly,[73] impartially,[74] comprehensively,[75] and publicly.[76] "Take no part in the unfruitful works of darkness, but instead expose them."[77] Ensuring things are biblically accurate is a scriptural command. But we need to stay away from having a critical spirit, as that can be damaging as well.

The book of Acts gives us an example of the Bereans and that:

> These were more noble than those in Thessalonica, in that they received the word with all readiness of mind, and searched the scriptures daily, whether those things were so.[78]

---

[71] 1 Corinthians 5:12–13 (NIV)

[72] 1 Corinthians 14:29

[73] John 7:24

[74] Leviticus 19:15

[75] 1 Thessalonians 5:20–22

[76] Scialdone, Tony, "Should Christians Judge People?" GodWords, accessed November 25, 2023, https://godwords.org/should-christians-judge-people/?utm_source=substack&utm_medium=email.

[77] Ephesians 5:11 (ESV)

[78] Acts 17:11 (KJV)

The idea that hiding things, not saying things in public, and not mentioning names, does not really line up with the Bible. Public sin requires public correction. Proverbs tells us:

> He that rebuketh a man afterwards shall find more favor than he that flattereth with the tongue.[79]

Paul publicly rebuked Peter in Antioch. He wrote to Timothy:

> As far those who persist in sin, rebuke them in the presence of all, so that the rest may stand in fear.[80]

Paul lists a half dozen false teachers by name, including Phygelus, Hermogenes, Demas, Hymenaeus, Philetus, and Alexander. Jesus, Paul, Luke, and John provide countless warnings about false teachers. Speaking truth is never tearing down the church but rather restoring it toward righteousness. Truth is going to build God's church and restore his people. And it is in this truth where we can find freedom, peace, and God's love.

---

[79] Proverbs 28:23
[80] 1 Timothy 5:20 (ESV)

9

The Good Church

You would be surprised at how cold it can get in Louisiana in the wintertime. Something to do with the humidity and the driving wind makes a cold morning seem so much worse. I heard one Louisiana resident stating he needed multiple layers of clothes to handle a winter Louisiana morning at 30 degrees, but he handled a 30-degree Chicago day in a T-shirt. I arrived at New Life Tabernacle church on one of those mornings, piercing bitter cold. The alligators were hiding, and no one was even thinking about going out to get some of that delicious Cajun or Creole food. Arriving at New Life Tabernacle a bit early, Pastor Tony Spell was not at the building. I was not expecting to actually be able to meet him.

But then Pastor Tony rolled up. He was driving one of his buses. The church runs fifteen buses every Sunday morning along various routes. They pick up poor and disadvantaged kids in these buses, take them to the church, feed them a full breakfast, let them play some basketball if they arrive early, and then provide them with a full gospel curriculum. If you have ever had any experience in the inner-city school system, it does not take long to feel the depression, isolation, desperation, fear, and a sense that you are trapped in a prison with no chance to escape.

Hope and education are what the kids need. It was what was taken away from them. That is what is provided to these children on Sunday mornings. These children do not have transportation or much to offer financially. Oftentimes the parents do not even go to church. The young children get dressed and ready to go all by themselves while their parents are sleeping. After all, this is the day of the week they have been waiting for. Pastor Tony reminds us that the point of the church is to reach out to the poor, helpless, and disadvantaged because "they that are well are in no need of a physician."[81] The lifestyle of these children and what they have to encounter is rough, but people have survived challenging situations before. All they need is a little bit of hope, and that is what they get when they see Pastor Tony's buses rumbling down the street on Sunday morning.

Pastor Tony Spell rose to national attention during the COVID crisis. COVID terrified the nation. The media made it clear that the only way to survive COVID was to live in fear and hide in your basement with multiple masks on. Other people tried other approaches. They would go outside in the fresh air, exercise, take vitamins, and strengthen their immune system. And many ended up surviving COVID just fine, but they became the enemies of the media. But Pastor Tony was not here to get involved in the COVID narrative. He just knew that he woke up at 5:00 a.m. every Sunday morning to change people's lives, and he was not going to stop now because the guy on CNN told him to. He said that they had too much momentum going from the decades of running the church, activities, and the bus program to quit now based on the demands from the guy on the TV set.

Every church had its own policy on COVID. Many churches closed, and many did not, some even growing in size. But Pastor Tony Spell caught the attention of the news media, and they would not leave him alone. Pastor Tony refused to budge on his First Amendment rights to not prohibit his free exercise of religion.[82] He

---

[81] Matthew 9:12

[82] Before agreeing to accept the Constitution, the founders demanded that these freedoms be protected by an amendment to the original document—the First Amendment which states, "Congress shall make no law respecting an establishment of religion, or prohibiting the free exercise thereof; or abridging the freedom of speech, or of the press; or the right of the people peaceably to assemble, and to petition the government for a redress of grievances."

got arrested and was put under house arrest with orders to not leave his house. But on Sunday morning, Pastor Tony left his house and headed to his church to preach every Sunday like he always has. He went with his ankle monitor on. The media went nuts. They said that he died of COVID, his wife died of COVID, his church members died of COVID, and that Pastor Tony was out running people over with his buses. But no one died of COVID, and no one got ran over. In fact, as other churches became shut down, and due to the national attention, this was bringing, his online viewership swelled to half of a million people.

When Pastor Tony Spell talks about what makes a good church in his hypnotic rhythmic style, he says that in today's terminology, many people think of a large building, beautiful edifice, stained glass windows, padded pews, plush carpet, or an updated sound system. When we say a great church, many mean a large building or much wealth. Look at all the wealth they have obtained and many churches. Look at what they can do for the community, diversity of members, large membership, influence, and prestige. Maybe Oratorical excellency from a silver-tongued preacher. Pastor Tony boldly declared, "What makes a great church? Jesus Christ and Him crucified makes a great church."

Pastor Tony states that a good church is a witnessing church. "We were great while they were small, and they were small where we were great." A great church will have great power. A great church will be a witnessing church, not a lot of dreaming and scheming but witnessing. A good church talks about the resurrection. There will be hope, health, deliverance, and joy. He warns us about focusing on being a better us. We are wrapped up in *me, myself,* and *I*—but it's all about Jesus, If I'm good, it's about Jesus. If I'm successful, it's about Jesus. If something right happens, it's about Jesus.

Pastor Tony also reminds us that a great church has great grace. A gracious church does not come to condemn but does come to convict you today. A great church has great fear. Trust in the Lord with all thine heart and lean not on your own understanding. Fear God but not man. A great church has great persecution. Dead churches will comply; the early church that swept the Roman world with a strange joy thrived on persecution and tribulation.

A great church has great joy. It took one night to get Israel out of Egypt but forty years to get Egypt out of Israel. God can deliver you in a moment's time. Anyone can shout with money in the bank, but can you shout without it? A great church has trouble, more trouble than anybody, but they have joy about it. A great church has great results. You shall know them by their fruit. Acts 6:11 says, "A great number believed."[83] Pastor Tony Spell tells of a story of a man sitting alone in the dark filled with depression, discouragement, and despair. He was at the end of his rope and had a 12-gauge in his mouth, ready to leave the pain of this world behind. Then someone knocked on his door to tell him the good news about Jesus. He found hope. He put the gun away and ended up becoming a Sunday school teacher in the church.

Sometimes it does not get any simpler than that. Pastor Tony remarked that the church is not a club, the NFL is a club, and the church's job is to transform lives. Many churches today are partly good and partly bad. The true church is going to bring men to Jesus. They are going to see Jesus. It is not about smoke machines, fog machines, or lights. It is about Jesus. "Keep the main thing the main thing." It is not your gospel, but it is His gospel. Everyone should feel welcome but not always comfortable. A preacher's job is to convict people of sin. To complain about a preacher making you uncomfortable is like complaining about a dictionary having too many words.

It is not about Buddha, Krishna, or anyone else, but it is about Jesus, and if Jesus is there, it is a great church (John 14:6, John 10:1). If you come in some other way, you are a thief or a robber. Pastor Tony Spell reminds us that Jesus had twenty-five thousand listening to him at one time, and then he was down to twelve; it is not always about numbers. Finances do not always make things successful. Jesus pulled money out of a fish. Money does not matter; being sanctified does not matter, but Jesus matters. Bring men to Jesus; a great church

---

[83] Acts 11:21

is an outreaching church. Pastor Tony reminds us that God will have a church on this Earth, a true church.

On the opposite end of the country, Pastor Dale Gooding preaches out of Hunters Creek Church in Metamora, Michigan. Michigan could be one of the most underrated states in America. Surrounded by the great lakes, you have unlimited clean, clear, brisk water for fishing, swimming, and water sports. On the Lake Huron side, you have rocky shorelines and islands as the deep blue water mixes with the orange of the sun setting. On the other side, you have golden sand beaches and in some areas huge sand dunes that rise out of this vast freshwater ocean. In between, you have forests, streams, and lakes that belong to the hunters and fishermen. Apple orchards are plentiful along with the occasional wild apple tree or raspberry patch. If you ever get bored and want something different, you can take a bridge to the "UP" which is basically a grown-up version of some type of outdoor adventure wilderness amusement park.

Pastor Dale recommends the book *9 Marks of a Healthy Church*.[84] Pastor Dale says that there is a fine line between leadership and lordship. It is a line that a lot of pastors have a hard time with. Pastor Dale talks about expositional preaching which is based on the diligent study and careful exegesis of a passage. Scripture gets proclaimed as God's divinely inspired word.

> Preach the word; be ready in season and out
> of season; reprove, rebuke, and exhort, with com-
> plete patience and teaching.[85]

Expositional preaching takes the meaning out of the text versus topical preaching. Topical preaching can be good, but oftentimes, it can lead to error, and it becomes what you actually say versus what you should say. In some cases, topical teaching can be beneficial, but in other cases, it is leading people.

---

[84] Mark Dever
[85] 2 Timothy 4:2 (ESV)

Pastor Dale worries about pragmatism, which deals with things that are practical and sensible but maybe not theological. This leads to introducing what the people want but not necessarily what they need. Sermons become an inch deep and a mile wide.

Pastor Dale states that it is not really his responsibility to grow the church; it is God's job. He has noticed a trend across America, which is that many churches are afraid to be biblically based because of the cost. Pastor Dale noted that the Western church has a tendency to rely on the state for its liberty and mission. And that can be dangerous. We have the Constitution, which is a beautiful document and gives us our rights, and we should stand on those rights. But just remember that we do not gather because of the Constitution. We gather 'cause God says to, not due to the constitution. We gather due to the scriptures. Pastor Dale reminds us about other countries such as China. If we capitulate to the government because they tell us to, what happens down the road?

Pastor Dale says that a good church is going to proclaim the gospel message. Christ-centeredness is in the entire Bible. In every text, it all points to the gospel. It is a real need. It draws people's attention to the satisfaction of the gospel. The gospel is not just about salvation; it is the way of life. Abstain and give because of who and what Christ has called me to in His life, death, and resurrection. There is life as a new person is Christ. Evangelism will always point to Christ. You have to be explicit; you cannot beat around the bush. In an emphatic way, you have offended God. We have the shedding of blood offering of the body, resurrection of the son, and a demonstration of God's approval. We need an explicit, emphatic, intentional aspect of the gospel. What Christ has delivered us from is not just hell but God's judgment. We must satisfy this to remove this judgment and punishment; hell is just a destination.

Pastor Dale reminds us that we cannot neglect the Lord's command to intentionally disciple people. Disciple accountability, spiritual growth, scripture memorization, etc. To disciple someone, you first need to spend time with them. Get in the word, have personal accountability and form groups. Go over scriptures, explain them, apply them, and respond to them.

What happens if you go to an unhealthy church? First of all, why do you go there? Does it have some things that you want? Is it the denomination that you grew up in? Geographical preferences? Are you getting frustrated or convicted about what you see in the church? If not, should you be? Pastor Dale says the first step is to pray. The next step is to voice some concerns and see what to do next. Visit some other places and visit several times. Look at the church's constitution. Sit down with the pastor. And then pray some more. Even if you do find a great church, it could be the greatest church in the area. Maybe it is not for you. God's will might be for you to strengthen another church.

Heading even further up north in our hunt to find what makes a good church we have Alaska. Alaska is a very unique state. While it borders rural Canada, it is cut off from mainland America so everything flies in from Seattle, operating almost like an island. The beauty is stunning. I remember standing in a valley in one location. It seemed as if I could spot a waterfall everywhere that I looked. Glacial lakes, majestic mountains, and picturesque views make up the state. Summers are warm and full of adventure. In Fairbanks, the land of the midnight sun, they play a baseball game under the midnight sun, as it is sunny twenty-four hours a day for part of the summer.

Winters are the opposite extreme. They can be harsh, brutal, dark, cold, and unforgiving. The sun does not even come out for part of the winter in some parts of the state. Outside the main cities, the state is isolated from itself during the winter. Isolation can lead to depression and anxiety, and in many cases death, if medical attention cannot be reached. Planes are commonly used as a mode of transportation. Even the state's capital is cut off from the highway. The state picks up a lot of independent people who generally love to hunt with a Libertarian streak. While Alaska as a whole is cut off from the mainland, Kodiak Island, a large island off the Southern coast of Alaska, is even more isolated, as it is cut off from the main part of Alaska.

It is here that we can find Pastor Matt Altman. Kodiak Island is home to him, and he gets to enjoy the intensely beautiful summers with water, whales, mountains, bison, fish, and bears while enduring the harsh winters. What he also endures is the reality of the island around him. When he arrived, this island was more secularized and isolated than many areas on the mainland. Mental health and depression take a toll on some, due to the remoteness, darkness, and cold of the winters.

It is in this environment where Pastor Matt Altman runs his church. He believes it is imperative to set a proper foundation, which is the exaltation of Jesus Christ, and evangelize to the Glory of God. He reminds us that the church exists to bring glory to Christ, and everything springs out of that including equipping the saints for works of ministry and providing a safe, doctrinally strong place for the believers. He cautions us that churches can generally run into three ditches. The first is when your focus becomes all on the seekers and not exalting Christ. He says that everyone focuses on seekers and bringing people to some extent, but when that becomes your primary focus, your roots are not running deep, and you are built on a faulty foundation. You need to exist to reach people for the glory of God.

The second ditch that some churches run into is making their purpose to provide a good social network. An emotional and social network is good and is a part of the function of the church, but a good church needs more than self-help and pop psychology. The third ditch that some churches run into is that they may build truth but are scared of engaging with the outside world. They create some type of holy huddle and become hostile to the outside world.

Pastor Matt personally falls into the noncharismatic or less charismatic camp. What he notices is that there is a lack of concern, knowledge, and caring about spiritual warfare. But this is something that he reminds us of all Christians need to be concerned about whether they are in or out of the charismatic camp, as spiritual warfare is clearly listed in the Bible. He also warns us about materialism which is invading the church and the overindulgence of food, which is socially acceptable in many churches but can lead to gluttony.

Heading South back into the continental United States in our hunt for what makes a good church, we can find Pastor Paul L. Di Toma in New Life Church in Ohio. Ohio does not have as many outdoor recreational opportunities as some of the other states. But you have Lake Erie in the North with Put-In-Bay and Cedar Point. And as you get closer to the West Virginia side of the state, it gets more scenic with Hocking Hills State Park and other opportunities. Ohio is very interesting from a historical perspective. Eight US Presidents came from Ohio, more than any other state, and it is also home to the Wright brothers.

It is also associated with Charles Finney, who taught as a professor in Ohio and preached in Ohio and other states. He helped lead the second great awakening which urged followers to reject sin and lead morally upstanding lives which greatly impacted Ohio along with other states. The Second Great Awakening focused on the elimination of sin and led to transformed lives but also impacted some social justice issues such as temperance,[86] women's rights, and slavery abolition.[87] This, of course, was a continuation of the original great awakenings led by Jonathan Edwards and George Whitefield that followed the same formulas, repenting of sin, turning to God, and living a transformed life.

Pastor Paul says that some key formulas for a good church are team or shared leadership. You want an elder-led church of godly servant leaders who are committed to the inerrancy and infallibility of the Scriptures and to expository preaching. The people of the church need to have a hunger for this and a genuine love for God and the people. Be hospitable, warm, and welcoming, especially to those who are not yet Christian, a commitment to an authentic Christian community and biblical fellowship. A good church will take the Great Commission seriously and have a solid strategy to make disciple-making disciples. A good church reproduces disciples.

People regularly share their grace stories and the gospel as a way of life, give generously to the Lord's work, and support and send missionaries. People need to understand the importance of prayer and

---

[86] Americans above the age of fourteen on average consumed between 6.6 and 7.1 gallons of pure alcohol during this time period. (In 1998, Americans drank 2.8 gallons per year on average.)

[87] *Library of Congress - Constitutional Rights Foundation.* The Second Great Awakening and Reform in the 19th Century. (n.d.). Retrieved March 1, 2023, from https://www.crf-usa.org/images/pdf/the-second-great-awakening.pdf.

faithfully pray according to God's will and worship in Spirit and in truth. Leadership needs to make sure everything is Scripture-driven and honors God. Pastor Paul mentioned that a good church needs accountability with healthy people speaking the truth in love. He concluded with involvement in the community and finding ways to serve and witness.

When asked to address one troubling concern that he saw in the church today, Pastor Paul provided an entire list! So we will stick with a few of the more prominent ones. This would include liberalism and that core Christian beliefs are no longer held among church attendees. Such as the doctrines of sin, hell, the deity of Christ, and a biblical foundation in the Word of God. He also listed biblical illiteracy, moral failures, egalitarianism, lack of charity, watering down the gospel to draw a crowd, and a focus on perceived felt needs rather than actual needs addressed in Scripture.

It does seem that one mark of a good church is bearing fruit and seeing transformed lives. I once met a man who was one of the most excited, happy, energetic, and enthusiastic men I have ever seen. He seemed to dance about as he walked about. He was an older man but seemed as if he had some youthful energy pulsing through him. While talking to him, I could not help but notice a scar on his throat. I glanced at it a few times; he must have noticed that and brought it up. He said he sliced his throat from ear to ear. You do not really hear that much. Then he told me his story. He tried everything to find happiness. He tried all the usual things that are supposed to find pleasure in this world. He even tried God and church and would pray but still could not find peace. He chased and chased and chased and found nothing.

One day, he went back to his house, cut his throat from ear to ear, and slashed his wrists. That was it. He laid back on his bed to die. But someone was concerned about him and called the hospital. They rushed him into surgery. And he finally had reached the point where he cried out to God. He was beyond the end of his rope. And that is when God transformed his life. He was now heading in a new direction that would leave behind the depression, anger, and misery to walk in God's peace, love, and joy. His message is that Jesus can miraculously transform anyone and that your life, no matter how bleak things may look, can also be turned upside down through the power of God.

10

The Journey Ends

"What makes a good church? Jesus Christ and Him crucified makes a good church." Pastor Tony Spell summarizes things nicely with this statement. And while there are all different types of churches across America, some have elaborate worship time including dancing and others quietly hum hymns. Some have large commercial modern buildings and others are in a little church in the countryside. Some may disagree on more minor points of theological doctrine. But despite the differences, they are still united through Christ, the gospel message, and on a solid foundation with the Bible.

Pastor Lance Gentry from Cross and Crown Church can be found more toward the middle of the country, in skiing paradise, in Colorado, and brings in a few additional points on what a good church needs. Pastor Lance reminds us that the church is not his, or the elders, pastors, or members. It belongs to the Lord Jesus Christ. He gets to decide what is important; it is not our agenda and priorities. He will build our church. He is going to build; our job is to submit to him and love him.

When the Lord is listened to, He is given a central place in the church, and align under His leadership. Pursue the glory of God. We are called to declare the gospel. God is the creator, and man has fallen into sin. Jesus Christ is the only savior of mankind for all who place their faith and trust in Him. Maintain the centrality of scripture; answers are only found in His word. Keep the word central. He can rule and reign through His word. Keep scripture central and let the Lord rule the church. Tune the engine and set the compass. If you start with what people want, this is not a true compass. Set the compass to the scriptures and what the Lord wants. Do not set out to be an attractional church. We are not creating a brand. When you sell perfume, you are creating a brand. We are proclaiming the truth to the world.

To make sure that the compass is set in the right direction, Pastor Lance uses the Bible as his foundational measuring stick and also relies on the historic creeds, covenants, and declarations. If you go to his website, they are prominently displayed. The church affirms the EFCA Statement of Faith, Apostles' Creed, Cambridge Declaration, Chicago Statement, Nicene Creed, and Danvers Statement, and they have their own statement of faith. These statements of faith, declarations, creeds, and covenants are affirmed by all the pastors, teachers, and elders of the church because a strong foundation is imperative to the health and spiritual vitality of the church. Without sound doctrine, a church may be many things, but it will not be healthy.

Pastor Lance talks about anchoring beliefs in historic confessional Christianity. Do not forget Acts chapter 2. The church is over two thousand years old. That is two thousand years of faith, belief, and hammering out difficult doctrines. They said what they said carefully under difficult circumstances. There is no need for fresh ideas and statements. This is what Christians have always believed. They serve as helpful guardrails for the church. A good church needs to rediscover the ancient confessions and affirm them.

Similar to the creeds, we have the five solas, which launched the entire Protestant movement, which is basically every church outside the Catholic Church: *Sola scriptura, sola fide, sola gratia, sola Christo,* and *soli Deo gloria. Sola scriptura* means in God's word alone. The Bible itself is the highest source of authority in a Christian's life, the final court of appeal.

Sola fide means faith alone, which affirms that justification or being made right with God only comes through faith in Jesus. *Sola gratia* or grace alone says sinners are saved as an unearned gift of God's grace, not a result of works or payment to the church. *Sola*

Christo is Christ alone, emphasizing the exclusivity of the Cross of Christ's claim to salvation. And *soli Deo gloria*, is the glory of God alone, as the purpose of salvation, creation, and everything is for the Glory of God alone. Today, in some areas, the Protestant movement needs another reformation to reestablish these basic principles.

Another church that tries to live out these foundational principles is Grace Bible Church out of Montana. Montana is a state with some intense beauty. From Glaciers, lakes, forests, and open plains to mountain peaks, it really has the outdoor adventurist covered. Home to eight national parks, it includes some of the most famous national parks in America, including Glacier National Park, Yellowstone National Park, and Bighorn Canyon Recreation Area. It is a land of hiking, fresh air, and adventure. It is also home for Pastor Bryan Hughes from Grace Bible Church.

Pastor Bryan believes that God's word is central and foundational and preaches through the books of the Bible which provides a double protection from anyone looking to ride their hobby horse through the church or who has an ax to grind. He says that it also protects him from people who may accuse him of picking on them. He is just declaring what the Bible says. Pastor Bryan says that the two essential benchmarks of the church are love and sound doctrine. It is like a river; you need both. Some of the deadliest churches may be spot on with the doctrinal statement, but if they have no love, they have no life. Feed the people and love the people. Pastor Bryan reminds us that the Pharisees started off with good intentions. God rebuked them for adding their own commandments in place of God's commandments. They were completely focused on the externals; they looked really good on the outside but had a problem with their heart.

Pastor Bryan reminds us of the Letter of Jesus in Revelation 3.

Behold, I stand at the door, and knock: if
any man hear my voice, and open the door, I will

come in to him, and will sup with him, and he
with me.[88]

Here Jesus is talking to the church. He has need of nothing
but is standing and knocking at the heart. Jesus is reminding us, "I
know that you are in a dead church. They have everything. They do
not need Me. I am not welcome there. But you can still have individual fellowship with Me." While there is no guarantee that you can
change the church, start with leadership and pray. And remember
that we are guaranteed individual fellowship with Jesus, even if we
do go to a dead or unhealthy church.

The letter of Revelation to the seven churches mentioned by
Pastor Bryan was also frequently brought up by many of the pastors being interviewed. While some parts of the book certainly lead
to different interpretations, there seems to be a consensus that the
seven churches at the start of the book refer to seven contemporary
churches in that time, and they also represent all churches of all ages
and the state of the church during the end-times.

The churches mentioned are as follows:

- The church in Ephesus—the apostolic church. Ephesus
  was the religious and commercial center of Asia. They are
  told:

  > I know your works, your toil and your
  > patient endurance, and how you cannot bear
  > with those who are evil, but have tested those
  > who call themselves apostles and are not, and
  > found them to be false. I know you are endur-
  > ing patiently and bearing up for my name's sake,
  > and you have not grown weary. But I have this
  > against you, that you have abandoned the love
  > you had at first.[89]

---

[88] Revelation 3:20 (KJV)
[89] Revelation 2:2–5 (ESV)

This church was actively engaged in the mission of Christ and fought false teachers, but they were instructed to repent and return to their first love.

- Smyrna, the martyr church—They are encouraged to persevere through the tribulation and stay faithful until death, and they will be given a *crown of life.* They are materialistically poor but rich in spiritual things. Polycarp among others was martyred here; this is the church under tribulation and persecution.

- Pergamos: This was a beautiful art-filled city settled along the Caicus River. It was also a center of worship for the pagan gods. This is the church that is settled in the world and dealing with fornication; they made both religious and moral compromises to blend in with the pagan influences that were surrounding them. However, they "Did not deny my faith."[90] And are told: "Therefore repent. If not, I will come to you soon and war against them with the sword of my mouth."[91]

- Thyatira—They are told that "I know your works,"[92] and then it lists love, works, service, faith, and patience; seems like a great place. But they allow a false prophetess named Jezebel, who would not repent, to roam around and deceive the people and lead them into compromise. "Behold, I will throw her onto a sickbed, and those who commit adultery with her I will throw into great tribulation, unless they repent of her works."[93] But "the one who conquers and who keeps my works until the end, to him I will give authority over the nations."[94]

---

[90] Revelation 2:13b (ESV)

[91] Revelation 2:16 (ESV)

[92] Revelation 2:19a (ESV)

[93] Revelation 2:22 (ESV)

[94] Revelation 2:26 (ESV)

– Sardis is brought up next. This church is asleep. They are dead, lifeless, and unrepentant.

Remember, then, what you received and heard. Keep it, and repent. If you will not wake up, I will come like a thief, and you will not know at what hour I will come against you.[95]

While this church is mostly a lost cause, there are a few people left.

Yet you have still a few names in Sardis, people who have not soiled their garments, and they will walk with me in white, for they are worthy.[96]

– Philadelphia: This is referred to as the church in revival; they are keeping the Word of God even though they have little strength. They get no condemnation.

I know that you have but little power, and yet you have kept my word and have not denied my name.[97]

– The church of Laodicea gets the final letter; they are in the final state of apostasy, a wealthy and industrious city. They are rich and believe they need nothing but are actually wretched, miserable, and poor. Sir William Ramsay called them the city of compromise. There is no acclamation here, only condemnation.

I know your works: you are neither cold nor hot. Would that you were either cold or hot! So,

---

[95] Revelation 3:3 (ESV)
[96] Revelation 3:4 (ESV)
[97] Revelation 3:8b (ESV)

because you are lukewarm, and neither hot nor
cold, I will spit you out of my mouth.[98]

Apparently lukewarm water was standard in this city, whether it was icy water from the mountains that became lukewarm by the time it traveled to them or water from the hot springs, that eventually turned lukewarm. The lukewarm state is mentioned three times here. There is hope at the end as it states:

As many as I love, I rebuke and chasten: be
zealous therefore, and repent.[99]

Many Pastors reiterated the need for the Bible to have a foundational role in the church. Pastor Ross Shannon from the First Baptist Church of Lapeer was one of them. He reminds us that the church needs accurate preaching of God's word. It needs the gospel. God's word is proclaimed with authority. God's word brings life. Biblical vocalization of the gospel leads to conversion and evangelization. It is how Christians grow healthy; too much of Christianity today is becoming more like the American dream as our goal becomes to go out and get our piece of the American pie. But Pastor Ross reminds us that we cannot look toward the American dream as our primary focus, but it has to be the authority of scripture as we look for qualified biblical teachers to shepherd those new in the faith. Feel deeply, think deeply, engage, study God's word, and internalize it as God's word becomes life. And always watch out for the slippery slope that can lead to legalism or lawlessness.

Today we have broken, hurt, and fractured churches across America as battle-scarred sheep wander the fields looking for substance, but some are left starving. Moral scandals might make the news, but it is the theological scandals that are breaking the sheep. We just witnessed a nationwide shutdown of churches, and in some

---

98 Revelation 3:15–16 (ESV)
99 Revelation 3:19b (KJV)

areas, with some churches, it made no difference. Recent history shows us the churches in Europe began apostatizing before the entire continent of Europe apostatized. The land that led the reformation, had Whitefield preach to large crowds in fields as far as the ear could hear, is now mostly a secular continent. America is following in her footsteps. As the church goes, so goes the nation.

Dead churches are littered across America. Some are abandoned with peeling paint and uncut lawns; the COVID crisis knocked many out. But some have the lawns cut and are freshly painted, but they are dead inside. Dead churches do not belong to a particular denomination, though some denominations have more than others. It is not a certain church size or location. But it is found in the people. Maybe another life group will help. Maybe a new series by the pastor or another new big activity. Maybe another program. But it would not, and it never does. And over time, death attracts death, and the vibrant people meander away. You are left with an old, decaying, dying institution. So they do fundraisers and make commitments and try to get excited. But until the power of God comes to shake up their lives, they will remain as they are—committed to the religious institution, rather than to Christ.

The Bible tells us:

> But though we, or an angel from heaven, preach any other gospel unto you than that which we have preached unto you, let him be accursed. As we said before, so say I now again, if any man preach any other gospel unto you than that ye have received, let him be accursed.[100]

It also says:

> For the time will come when they will not endure sound doctrine; but after their own lusts shall they heap to themselves teachers, having

---

[100] Galatians 1:8–9 (KJV)

itching ears; And they shall turn away their ears
from the truth, and shall be turned unto fables.[101]

In some places, that time is upon us now. Self-improvement and entertainment guide one arm of the church while wealth creation and greed steer the other arm, and the Bible is used to handpick verses to justify each movement. They are united on one front, the advancement of yourself, rather than that of the Gospel. We have churches that have abandoned the Almighty to bow their knee to the almighty dollar as they confuse the blessings of God for a pay-to-play system. We have churches that have abandoned the central point of the Bible, the gospel message, to focus on entertainment, felt needs, and self-improvement as they strive to be better versions of themself instead of better versions of Christ's followers.

We have those who have used the power of the pulpit to create extra-biblical rules as their authority is stamped all over the lives, freedoms, and direction of its members who may never see true freedom in Christ Jesus as they are shackled in the cellars of their institution. We have those who are searching for feelings, emotions, and experiences rather than truth, the gospel, and the Bible as they create their own new path in this choose-your-own-adventure journey. We have those who have blended the world's symbols, gods, and idols with Christianity as they seek to forge their own path, as Israel oftentimes did to their own peril as they sought to build their own nation outside God's providence.

We have those who want to hang on to every non-essential difference, division, or interpretation, as justification to set themselves apart from their brother in Christ. We have seen enough division in the church, whether that is based on race, socioeconomic status, or theological differences. The true church needs to come together and set differences aside, while still taking a concrete stance on essential doctrines.[102] Some buildings that call themselves churches are in real-

---

[101] 2 Timothy 4:3 (KJV)

[102] Some churches would not argue with you about essential doctrines such as Christ, the cross, repentance of sin, etc., and they may even have them buried in a website somewhere. They want to appease everyone and all faiths. But

ity tax-exempt money-making institutions. And anytime a church's theology stands in sharp contrast to the Bible and aligns more with Hollywood, that is going to be a problem.

And we have good churches all across America that provide a support structure while transforming lives and the community. They are pillars of strength that bring truth, the gospel, and hope to entire cities and across America providing food, clothing, shelter, and clean clothes to those without clothes, food, and shelter. Many churches have dramatically impacted the community as the church spreads out from the Sunday building to radicalize the community. Some pastors have honored their commitment to Christ as they have been bombarded by attacks from the world, inside the church, and sometimes from our own government.

Many have used scriptural truth to fight back at the culture and those from within their own church. Many churches have stayed committed to the truth of the Bible while Hollywood, the media, and oftentimes members of their own church encouraged them to head in another direction.

This book has focused on the attributes that make up a good church and the attributes that make up a bad church. But what happens if you have made some mistakes or went in the wrong direction for a period and want to get back on the right track? Pastor Jeff Countryman might be one of those people who can help provide insight into this. I first met Pastor Jeff Countryman at Cape Christian Church when I was down in Cape Coral for a few months. It is a neat area with Cape Coral, Pine Island, Matlacha, and Cayo Costa. Matlacha was recently hit pretty hard by a hurricane, as was Cape Coral, evidenced by all the blue tarps that you could see on roofs. It looked like a Smurf village. What was neat about Cape Christian was that they had a large nicely done playground in front of the church by the highway. Basketball courts, a small splash pad, and a nice kids' play area. The church invited the entire community

---

truth is not designed to be buried behind a website. By removing the cross, Christianity becomes more of a cultural thing, which you can take part in with or without the cross.

to the park with no obligation to attend the church; they hired staff to clean the play area.

Since the church was right there, some of those people started going to the church; it brought in a lot of people. Pastor Jeff was a dynamic and engaging pastor who had a lot of charisma. But while his sermons were fascinating, they were also biblically authoritative, covering various angles from apologetics to the cross. And between the exciting messages, energy, fun people, and playground, it made people want to come back. And that is what they did. The church started rapidly growing and Pastor Jeff became a real pillar in the community.

But behind all this excitement, there was just one problem. Pastor Jeff had a million dollars of medical debt attached to him left behind from a physically challenging athletic career and a health mis-diagnosis that he got in Canada.[103] And he started feeling entitled. The past churches that he worked at all grew, and he felt entitled to some of that money. His ministry career involved growing churches; he did it well and started to get a little prideful and resentful that he was not able to participate as much in the harvest portion of things. So he started doctoring receipts and keeping some of that money. He felt guilty and convicted about this but was able to justify it in his mind. When you run a growing church with thousands of people, there is no real accountability program. You are on top and every-thing looks good from the outside. He still loved God and wanted to serve him. He did this for months and felt convicted about it and felt like God told him that it was wrong; the Holy Spirit reminded him. But he was able to justify things.

By month 10, he had no worries or convictions, and this had become routine. He did it in a way no one would ever know. And besides, he deserved this money for growing this church and other churches, and he was good at what he did. At month 16, something different happened. He clearly felt like he heard God tell him that this was his last warning. It gave him pause. But he did it anyway. And then something different happened. He was immediately filled

---

[103] Yay! Socialized medicine

with fear, stress, and anxiety. He never experienced this before. But it was now part of his life. It was constant and would not go away. His world was about to be turned upside down.

When you are out late on the weekend and all the main people who run the church are at your house and say they are willing to wait there, even if you get home at midnight, it is not really a good sign. They knew and accused him of stealing. His wife passionately defended him: "How dare you accuse my husband of such a terrible thing." You see, she did not know. No one knew. But God knew. The way that this was done, it could have never been proven anyway. Circumstantial evidence. But Pastor Jeff had enough. He admitted it. He was done. And he was no longer Pastor Jeff anymore. Just Jeff.[104]

"Dad, you are on Fox News and ABC News." Soon pictures of him in an orange jumpsuit would be spread across America as criminal charges were being filed against him. What was once a secret was now national news.

Pastor Jeff mostly just stayed in his bed for the next three months. It was not until his wife told him that something needed to happen or else, they would not have a place to stay that prompted him to get a minimum-wage job to get some income. He spent his days just riding around on lawn equipment, crying, and praying.

Pastor Jeff embarked on a two-year restoration program with eight pastors that was pretty intense. No ministry or speaking, just restoration. He paid back the money that he stole. Criminal charges were dropped. He could not go to the grocery store without people noticing him, but the community got behind his restoration. He got a job helping another church with its marketing and online presence. Then he landed another job as a pastor. He has started speaking and teaching again, as he was designed to do. Pastor Jeff said, "It took about five years for this to become something that took place, not something that I am going through."

This is certainly not the first story of someone dropping the ball or doing something that they should not have. Many people

---

[104] Pastor Jeff was simultaneously working at two churches at the same time when this happened and was fired from both churches for the same reason.

think things would have been a lot easier if they had a chance to walk around with Jesus. More faith, more wisdom, more love. And it makes sense, after all, that they had a firsthand account of all these miracles, teachings, and excitement.

Yet Peter was one of those people. And when the going got tough, he was the first to deny Jesus, even though Jesus warned him that it would happen. When he realized his mistake, he went out and wept bitterly.[105] Yet the Bible says: "Upon this rock I will build my church."[106] Even though Peter was a failed person, God picked him up from those failures and decided that he would be the rock to build his church upon. Peter had true repentance and a heart that loved God. And after his original mistake, he never went back to that lifestyle and was so emboldened in the faith that he was eventually martyred in a similar fashion as Jesus, just upside down, because he felt that he was not worthy to have it done in the same manner as Jesus.

It seems to be less about perfection and more about a repentant heart and allowing God to work through you. David was a great man after God's own heart, yet he gave in to idleness which led to an affair and then murder. He repented and was later restored but had to deal with the tragic consequences of his sin, which he regretted for the rest of his life.

> Have mercy upon me, O God, according to thy lovingkindness: According unto the multitude of thy tender mercies blot out my transgressions. Wash me thoroughly from mine iniquity, And cleanse me from my sin.[107]

Gideon was supposed to be a "mighty man of valor"[108] and lead Israel against the battle against the Midianites yet he was found hiding in an old winepress because he was focusing on his circumstances and his fear, rather than what God promised. Where God

---

[105] Luke 22:62

[106] Matthew 16:18b (ESV)

[107] Psalm 51:1–4 (KJV)

[108] Judges 6:12 (ESV)

saw strength, Gideon felt weakness as the tail end of a small tribe. So he devised a series of tests, now commonly referred to as Gideon's fleece. In the end, Gideon heads in a new direction. He might still be the coward hiding in the winepress, but he was also a mighty warrior who led an army of three hundred Israelites to defeat the Midians in five hundred to one miraculous odds.

And then we have the entire nation of Israel. They fall away from God again and again. Then God sends in another enemy to oppress them. They cry out to the Lord, and God saves them. Then they go back to idolatry and sin, get trapped in bondage, get oppressed, and cry out to the Lord again who does deliver them. It seems that what God wants from us is not perfection but repentance and then to head in a new direction far from sin and our old life, a life of faith that overcomes sin and fear.

There are good churches and bad churches out there, just as there are good people and bad people. But there are also good people in bad churches, and bad people in good churches as we have the enemy knocking on the door of good churches. Pastor Curtis Suuppi from the Rising Church brings up the famous John F. Kennedy quote: "Ask not what your country can do for you—ask what you can do for your country." Pastor Curtis said the same thing can be applied to your church: "Ask not what your church can do for you—ask what you can do for your church." But perhaps we can take this one step further and look at it not as what Christ can do for you but as what you can do for Christ.

You cannot have a church without the gospel. You can have a big social club, like a giant rotary club. You can hand out titles, clap for people, and even have a great time with it, but you cannot really have a church. You can create a tax-free institution to launder money to yourself, but you cannot really have a church. There have been no effective Christian campaigns that hid the gospel message, in order to proclaim the gospel message. You can create a large institution and bring in millions of dollars and sell books and become famous, and be on talk shows, but you cannot have a church without the gospel.

History has not only given us the extreme example of a bad church in Adolf Hitler but another extreme example in Dietrich

Bonhoeffer. Many churches in America are found between these extremes. For most places, the term *bad church* may be a bit coarse. Maybe the term *unhealthy church* is a better fit. In other places, we have good churches that may have gotten a little off track. In some areas, we have good churches that need to continue heading in that direction and, in some cases, encouraging other churches to head down that same path. Regardless of how you categorize certain churches, we can see that several churches need to head in a new direction where, in many places, change is needed. And more often than not, the change that we need to see in the church today, the change needed to restore America, is not going to happen from one of these historical figures, but it needs to happen with you. *Soli Deo Gloria.*

I would like to thank these churches and pastors who somehow helped with the process (partial list):

- Alabama: Christ City Church, SonRise Baptist Church, Grace Covenant Baptist Church, Cross Creek Church, Dr. Chris Peters
- Alaska: Radiant Church, Valley Bible Chalet, Berean Baptist Church-Pastor Matt Altman, Christian Community Church
- Arizona: Costi Hinn-Shepherd's House Bible Church, Christ's Church of Tucson-Dr. Dale Briggs, Hope Bible Church-Pastor Bill Borinstein
- Arkansas: Pastor Jason Vaden-Urban Harvest Fellowship
- California: Pastor Jack Hibbs-Creekside Bible Church, McKinleyville Baptist-Pastor Will O'Brien, Pastor Aaron Newman-Union Church, Dr. Goetsch
- Canada: Pastor Artur Pawlowski
- Colorado: Pastor Dan Harty-Windsor Community Church, Pastor David Talbert-Freedom in the Word Ministries, Cross and Crown Church Pastor Lance Gentry
- Connecticut: Pastor Landon Reesor-Christ Community Church
- Delaware: Rev. Josh Guzman-Crossroads Presbyterian Church, CenterPoint Church
- Florida: Dr. Mike Chandler-Grace Pointe Church Florida, Dr. Kirt Anderson-Naples Community Church Florida, Christ Fellowship
- Pastor Carlos Cardenas and Omar Giritli, Tom Ascol-pastor of Grace Baptist Church in Cape Coral, Grace Family Church, Ybor and Clearwater, Pastor Terry Smith-New Beginnings Tabernacle Missionary Baptist Church,

Bible Truth Ministries Tampa, Grace Bible Church of Tampa-Pastor Mike Sprott, Pastor Joel-Urban Church, Pastor David Dean-Cape Christian Church Cape Coral

- Georgia: Rev. Randy Forrester-St. Andrews Church, Dr. Brian Powell-Holy City Church
- Hawaii: Pastor James, Pastor Matt-Hawaii: Grassroots Church, Pastor John-Solid Rock East Hawaii, New Hope Fellowship, Puna Baptist Church, Sure Foundation Church
- Idaho: Creekside Bible Church, Kootenai Community Church-Pastor Jim Osman, Table Rock Church
- Illinois: Moody Bible Church, Jim Miller, Dr. Erwin Lutzer
- Indiana: Dustin Crawford-Cornerstone Community Church, The Connection: A Community Church-Charles Townsend
- Iowa: Grace Community Church
- Kansas: Community Bible Church
- Kentucky: Bowen First Church of God, Living Hope Baptist Church, Liberty Bible Church, Highview Baptist Church
- Louisiana: First Wego Church, Berean Bible Church-Pastor Tony Spell
- Maine: Harbor Light Church, The Church at Spruce Creek, Sheepscot Valley Community Church
- Maryland: Covenant Life Church-Pastor Kevin Rodgers, The Well Community Church-Pastor Matt Klinger
- Massachusetts: Pastor Jeff Oakes-Reunion Christian Church, Branch Church-Pastor Mason Adair
- Michigan: Pastor Lamar Black, Port Huron Church of Christ; Pastor Leo Robinson II, The Good Church; Pastor Ed, Pastor Keith Atwater, Pastor C. T. Eldridge, Woodside Church; Mount Zion Church; The Rising Church; Pastor Curtis Suuppi, Pastor Bob Holt, Pastor Jesse Holt, Christ the King Church; Pastor Todd Petty, Pastor Dale Gooding Hunters Creek Community Church; Rev. Bruce A. Shields, House of Faith Church; Pastor Jerry Theis,

Radiant Church; St. Paul Lutheran Church, Pastor Kevin Cook, Pastor Jon Waters, Pastor Reid

- Minnesota: Berean Baptist Church-Dr. Devin Macdonald, Mission Orthodox Presbyterian Church, Dr. Michael Seufert, Henry Bechthold
- Mississippi: Lifepoint Church-Pastor George Ross
- Missouri: Gospel Life Church
- Montana: Grace Bible Church-Pastor Bryan Hughes
- Nebraska: Ramel Williams of North Metro Bible Church
- Nevada: Pastor Brad Borowski of Living Stones, Pastor Kevin Scott of The Stream
- New Hampshire: New Frontiers Church
- New Jersey: Ocean City Baptist Church
- New Mexico: Hope Church, Mountain Valley Church-Pastor Chris Promersberger
- New York: New Creation Fellowship, Tottenville Evangelical Church
- North Carolina: Living Word Bible-Pastor Bob Grass
- North Dakota: Calvary Church-Pastor Ben Killerlain, Lighthouse Ministries
- Ohio: NewLife Church-Pastor Paul Di Toma
- Oklahoma: Pastor Tyler Wilson
- Oregon: Heritage Christian Fellowship-Pastor Jeremy Nehf
- Pennsylvania: Pastor Mike Anderson-City Light Church
- Philadelphia: New Life Presbyterian Church-Rev. Jared Nelson, Living Water Community Church-Pastor Mike Lorenzo
- Rhode Island: Grace Bible Church-Pastor Dan Crichton, Pastor Troy Edwards-Christ's Victory Bible Teaching Center
- South Carolina: Pastor Ryan Glosson-First Baptist Church in Turbeville South Carolina
- South Dakota: Emmaus Road Church-Pastor Matt Groen, New Life Evangelical Free Church-Pastor Michael Wallenmeyer
- Tennessee: Grace Community Church

- Texas: New Beginnings Longview-Pastor Daniel, Stonebriar Community Church-Pastor Chuck Swindoll, Pastor Steve Leblanc-Sherman Bible, Sunrise Community Church-Pastor Mark Hilbelink, Westwood Baptist Church-Pastor Rick Dees
- Utah: Refuge Church-Pastor Brian Suave, Gospel Hope Church
- Vermont: Pastor Ben Whittinghill
- Virginia: Pastor Gary Hamrick-Cornerstone Chapel Virginia, Washington Redemption Church-Pastor Matt Boswell
- West Virginia: The Church at Martinsburg-Pastor Patrick Flowers
- Wisconsin: First Baptist West Bend
- Wyoming: Meadowbrooke Church
- Washington DC: Capitol Hill Baptist Church-Pastor Mark Dever, 9Marks
- Quito: English Fellowship Church
- Keith Carroll-Literary Agent

Additional books based on this topic that may be beneficial:

- *Ten Indictments Against the Modern Church* by Paul Washer
- *9 Marks of a Healthy Church* by Mark Dever
- *The Prosperity Gospel: Gospel of Greed* by Jim Garnett
- *The Gospel Driven Church* by Matt Chandler
- *A Different Gospel* by D. R. McConnell
- *Beyond Seduction: A Return to Biblical Christianity* by Dave Hunt
- *Faith Undone* by Roger Oakland
- *The Saviour Sensitive Church* by Dr. Paul Chappell and Dr. John Goetsch
- *Deceived No More* by Doreen Virtue
- *Another Gospel* by Alisa Childers
- *God, Greed, and the Prosperity Gospel* by Costi Hinn
- *The Ten Commandments of Progressive Christianity* by Michael J. Kruger
- *Defining Deception* by Costi W. Hinn
- *Ashamed of the Gospel* by John MacArthur
- *An Apostate Church* by Billy Lauderdale
- *The Prodigal Church: A Gentle Manifesto against the Status Quo* by Jared C. Wilson
- *God, Greed, and the Prosperity Gospel* by Costi W. Hinn.
- *Blessed* by Kate Bowler
- *Health, Wealth, and Happiness How the Prosperity Gospel Overshadows the Gospel of Christ* by David W. Jones and Russell S. Woodbridge
- *A New Apostolic Reformation* by Douglas Geivett and Holly Pivec
- *The Prosperity Gospel, Gospel of Greed* by Jim Garnett

- *The Gospel-Driven Church: Uniting Church Growth Dreams with the Metrics of Grace* by Jared C. Wilson
- *Prosperity Seeking the True Gospel* Mbugua, Maura, Mbewe, Gruden, Piper
- *Learn to Discern Recognizing False Teachings in the Christian Church Today* by Daniel Plunkett
- *Beware of the New Apostolic Reformation* by A Sound Word Ministry Publication
- *God's Super-Apostles* by R. Douglas Geivett and Holly Pivec
- *A Hidden Path Bethel Redding and Beyond* by A Sound Word Ministry Publication
- *Prosperity Seeking the True Gospel* by Mbugua, Maura, Mbewe, Gruden, John Piper
- *Seeker Sensitive Doctrines that Can Take You to Hell* by Henry Bechthold
- *Suburbianity: What Have We Done to the Gospel? Can We Find Our Way Back to Biblical Christianity?* by Byron Forrest Yawn
- *A Wonderful Deception: The Further New Age Implications of the Emerging Purpose Driven Movement* by Warren B. Smith
- *The Dark Side of the Purpose Driven Church* by Noah W. Hutchings
- *Christianity in Crisis: 21ˢᵗ Century* by Hank Hanegraaff
- *Exposing Mega Churches and the Prosperity Gospel Scam*, Henry Bechthold
- *The Kingdom of the Cults* by Walter Martin
- *The Case for a Creator* by Lee Strobel
- *More Than a Carpenter* by Josh and Sean McDowell
- *The New Answers Book 1* by Ken Ham
- *Mere Christianity* by CS Lewis
- *Icons of Evolution* by Jonathan Wells
- *The Battle for the Beginning* by John MacArthur
- *I Do not Have Enough Faith to be an Atheist* by Norman L. Geisler and Frank Turek
- *Trilogy* by Francis Schaeffer

- *The Handbook of Christian Apologetics* by Peter Kreeft and Ronald K. Tacelli
- *The Genesis Flood* by John C. Whitcomb and Henry Morris
- *Beyond Seduction* by Dave Hunt
- *The Pursuit of God* by A. W. Tozer
- *Martin Luther* by Eric Metaxas
- *Jack Hayford* by The Beauty of Spiritual Language
- *Strange Fire* by John MacArthur
- *Hell's Best Kept Secret* by Ray Comfort
- *The Prodigal God* by Tim Keller
- *When a Nation Forgets God* by Erwin Lutzer
- *Knowing God* by J. I. Packer
- *God Has a Wonderful Plan for Your Life* by Ray Comfort
- *Beyond the 95 Theses* by Stephen J. Nichols
- *Christian Doctrine* by Shirley C. Guthrie
- *The Foundations of Christian Doctrine* by Kevin J. Conner
- *The Lie* by Ken Ham
- *Exposing Mega Churches and the Prosperity Gospel Scam: They Could Feed Every Starving Person Worldwide and House Every Homeless American* by Henry Bechthold
- *A Gentle Manifesto against the Status Quo: The Prodigal Church* by Jared C. Wilson
- *Canceled Science* by Eric Hedin
- *Rediscover Church: Why the Body of Christ is Essential* by Collin Hansen and Jonathan Leeman
- *Death of a Guru* by Rabi R. Maharaj
- *Fast Facts on False Teachings* by Ron Carlson and Ed Decker
- *My Life without God* by William J. Murray
- *Life in Hawaii* by Titus Coan
- *Radical* by David Platt
- *Paradise* by Mark Cahill
- *Out of the Devil's Cauldron: A Journey from Darkness to Light* by John Ramirez
- *Broken Faith* by Mitch Weiss
- *The Cross and the Switchblade* by David Wilkerson
- *American Gospel: Christ Alone* (movie)

"Beware of rebellion, lawlessness, and hobby horses. Sometimes a group will just start riding hobby horses…Whether this is end times, prophecy, or prosperity, you cannot focus on one thing and disregard others, this leads to unbalance."

—Pastor Keith Atwood, New
Beginnings Church, Michigan

"Some Christians are taught that emotions are bad, as a result of that, there can be an unhealthy atmosphere…Some churches have overcorrected this and have created environments where feeling good is what you are in pursuit of, it is the primary focus."

—Pastor Jeremy Neff, Heritage
Christian Fellowship, Oregon

"A division in some cases can be healthy, as long as you recognize that you are still one in the body of Christ."

—Pastor Aaron Newman, Union
Church, California

"The danger today is that we cannot focus so much on entertainment that we forget about the truth of his word…Bring a balance to the church. Some churches rely all on the Bible, which is good, but they reject the things of the Spirit. Other churches focus solely on the Spirit and experiences, but they reject the words of the Bible."

—Pastor Bruce Shields, Author,
Pastor, and Vice President of the Iosco
County Ministerial Association

"Focus on preaching from the pulpit and ignore cultural or political references. Politics can put a lot of pressure on you and lead to an abuse of the pulpit."

—Dr. Kirt Anderson, Naples
Community Church, Florida

"Strive to be perfect and Christlike, but when you do sin you have an advocate, and this advocate is the propitiation for the world."
—Pastor Ben Whittinghill,
Rivertown Church, Vermont

"With no absolute truth, the scriptures and the gospel are constantly redefined and deconstructed as the cultural climate changes. Core doctrinal truths get redefined as Jesus becomes more of a good moral teacher, rather than a redeemer from sin."
—Pastor Tyler Wilson, The Well
Church, Oklahoma

"If you start with what people want, this is not a true compass, set the compass to the scriptures and what the Lord wants."
—Pastor Lance Gentry, Cross and
Crown Church, Colorado

"The two essential benchmarks of the church are love and sound doctrine. It is like a river, you need both. Some of the deadliest churches may be spot on with the doctrinal statement but if they have no love, they have no life."
—Pastor Bryan Hughes, Grace
Bible Church, Montana

"What makes a great church, Jesus Christ and him crucified makes a great church."
—Pastor Tony Spell Life Tabernacle
Church, Baton Rouge, Louisiana

"There is a fine line between leadership and lordship."
—Pastor Dale Gooding, Hunters Creek
Community Church, Michigan

"Set a proper foundation, which is the exaltation of Jesus Christ and evangelize to the Glory of God."

—Pastor Matt Altman, Berean
Baptist Church, Alaska

"A good church reproduces disciples."

—Pastor Paul L. Di Toma,
New Life Church, Ohio

"A good church seeks to shine the glory of God while dimming the light of man."

—Pastor Joel, Urban Chapel, Ybor